Prophecy and Prophets

December, 2016

Richard Oswald Commey

Copyright © 2007 Richard Oswald Commey

ISBN: 1-933899-71-9

Published by:
Holy Fire Publishing
Unit 116
1525-D Old Trolley Rd.
Summerville, SC 29485

www.ChristianPublish.com

Printed in the United States of America and the United Kingdom

Dedication

To all the called, the chosen, and the faithful prophets of God.

1. Remember whenever somebody is held in spiritual bondage, there are demons involved and those demons must be wrestled with. That is why we have to wrestle with and defeat demons through the power that is in the blood of Jesus, through the Word of God and by the power of the Holy Spirit 63-64

2. Anything that happens in the Spiritual World eventually happens in the physical World. Once the spiritual problem is dealt with in the Spiritual World, then we will see everything resolved in the natural 65

3. Prophecy is a minor role. The main part is raising people saints. Of course prothecy is an integral part of equipping but it is not the main part 117

4. THE GIFT OF DISCERNING OF SPIRITS is the supernatural ability to see into the spiritual realm. To discern something is to know something either by seeing or hearing in the spirit world 137, 139

TRANCE: This is when a person sees into the spirit world and the entire physical environment is suspended. Peter had a trance before preaching to Cornelias household Acts 10:9-16. In a trance all things around you will vanish. You may not see items around you, such as chairs, tables, but you will be more concious of the spiritual world 138

Acknowledgements

There are a number of people who were instrumental in making this book possible and without whose help this book will not have seen the light of day.

First of all, I thank the Almighty God who gave me the wisdom and knowledge to be able to write this book.

To my wife Babsi, your immeasurable support in my ministry has made the writing of this book a reality. You have been a wonderful helper, and a homemaker. I am very grateful.

To my publisher, Holy Fire publishers, I appreciate your invaluable support and encouragement during the publishing phase of this book. You made it happen!
Thank you very much.

To Dr. Vanessa Tetteh for your editorial and proofreading ability. Your editing and proofreading of my book demands commendation. I highly appreciate your work.

To Cyril Heymann, You are really a man after God's heart! Your passion to see the truth about prophecy put on paper caused you to support this project financially, and not only that, you threw your media weight behind me to make sure I had interviews with top media houses to teach the church the right operation of the prophetic ministry.

Table of Contents

Preface

Dear friends, I believe my calling as a prophet and a teacher is to enlighten the body of Christ about the prophetic ministry. I have been doing this for many years: as a matter of fact, when I was twenty years old and newly born-again, I received this supernatural endowment - I believe from Christ Jesus, the head of the Church. The Lord spoke to me in an audible voice. He said, "My son, I am calling you as a prophet to nations". I went on after that to study engineering at university. I graduated in 1987 and travelled to a few countries. All along, I had been conducting a vast amount of research on the subject of prophecy. I later did my Bachelor's degree in Theology, a Masters, and a Doctorate in Biblical Studies, with the latter two focusing on prophecy. I did this because I knew that it had something to do with my life's calling, which the Lord was calling me to be established in this particular ministry.

I did a lot of studying, read all the books available on the market at the time, and followed the prophets of the day. By the grace of God, I was called by God to leave my engineering profession in 1995, giving up a lucrative career in the United States as a research engineer. In 1995, the Lord told me to go to Ghana to plant a church and teach on prophecy. I stayed in Ghana for ten years, up to 2004, when the Lord relocated me to the United Kingdom to start another work, in the form of a church and a School of Ministry for training leaders and prophets.

As you know, the prophetic ministry is a very powerful and very important ministry in Christendom, but unfortunately, we don't know much about the prophet. Prophets have been, as the Bible states in Luke 1:67-70, since the world began, but at a stage in church history, prophetic ministry vanished from the scene. To use an ecological term, it became *extinct*.

Since the early 1980s, there has been a restoration or re-emergence, of the prophet. I believe that I am one of the many that God is calling to teach on the subject and bring training, equipping and mentoring to the younger ones who are coming up in this ministry. That is why I write this book at this time: ministers and others in this ministry may find its contents useful as a training manual.

In this book we shall discuss what prophecy is and define its limits. We shall also look at the history of the prophetic movement – where it all began, as far as Christian ministry is concerned. Then we will look at modes (methods and ways) of prophetic receptivity. Here I will share how prophetic words are received and how we can know whether these words are valid.

Next, we shall review different levels of prophetic activity. For instance, now in the New Testament church, every born-again Christian has the Spirit of God, because in Romans 8:9 we are told that if you don't have the Spirit indwelling you, then you are not a *bona fide* Christian. We will see that although we may all be Christians with the Holy Spirit dwelling in us, we are all not prophetic to the same degree. There are different levels of prophetic anointing, or ability.

We shall also look at the nature and character of the prophetic word. Among others, this has to do with the power that is embedded in the prophetic word - the fact that the prophetic word itself is creative, may be conditional, and so on. There are many things that we need to know about prophecy.

We shall also look at the management of prophecy. When you get a prophecy, what must you do? Many people receive prophecies, but they don't know how to process the words that they have received.

We will also find out how we ought to judge the prophetic word and the prophetic vessel. When you get a prophecy, it must be tested in order for you to be sure that the words came from God, because there are many other voices in the world, according to 1 Corinthians 14:10.

Finally we will look at the prophetic office. We will ask questions like: *Who is a prophet?* We want to find out the answer from the biblical perspective. If anyone comes to you and says that he or she is a prophet or a prophetess, does it really mean that he or she truly is so, insofar as the bible is concerned? We need to know who God says is a prophet, not who says he is a prophet, and not who men say is a prophet. We need a standard of judgment.

I must say that this teaching is not put together to attack, criticise or condemn. God has called me as a prophet to nations, to teach about prophecy, to educate - even other prophets, and to raise young prophets who may not be doing the right thing at this moment. We all make mistakes. I myself am still studying and learning more things: no one has got it all. Paul says in Philippians 3:13-4:

> "Brethren, I do not count myself to have apprehended; but one thing I do, forgetting those things which are behind and reaching forward to those things which are ahead, I press toward the goal for the prize of the upward call of God in Christ Jesus."

Rev. Dr. Richard Oswald Commey

Chapter 1:

Definition of Prophecy

What is prophecy? In Greek, the language in which the New Testament was written, the word *Prophecy* can be broken down into two words, *Pro* and *Phemi*. *Pro* means "forth" and *Phemi* means "to speak". Prophecy therefore means, "to speak forth". So prophecy has got to do with speech and voice – saying something.

Essentially:

> **Prophecy is the speaking forth of the mind and the counsel of God.**

True prophecy originates from God. Remember, if you are born-again, God is your father - God who created all things and knows all things about everything. Often, God wants to reveal to us His mind and His counsel. The Bible declares in Jeremiah 29:11:

> *"For I know the thoughts that I think toward you, says the LORD, thoughts of peace and not of evil, to give you a future and a hope."*

Since God knows everything, and we, being limited, don't know everything, the only way God can make known His thoughts to us is by revelation. And many times, revelation comes in the form of speaking: God speaking His mind through a human instrument or a vessel.

1a.   Word studies relating to prophecy

We have seen various noun forms portraying different aspects of prophecy. As we have already established, prophecy is the forth telling of the will of God, whether with reference to the past, the present or the future. It can also be said to be the declaration of God's message under the influence of His Spirit. It is a supernatural utterance in a language known by the speaker.

From these definitions we get to understand that when we prophesy, we are not speaking from our mind or intellect what we know, as seen in 2 Peter 1:19-21:

> *"And so we have the prophetic word confirmed, which you do well to heed as a light that shines in a dark place, until the day dawns and the morning star rises in your hearts; knowing this first, that no prophecy of Scripture is of any private interpretation, for prophecy never came by the will of man, but holy men of God spoke as they were moved by the Holy Spirit."*

The Bible states, *"...for prophecy never came by the will of man..."* (2 Peter 1:21). This means that those who give prophecies should not just think up something to say, but prophecy should come – and indeed, comes - as described in 2 Peter 1:21:

> *"...but holy men of God spoke as they were moved by the Holy Spirit".*

The word *holy* here, *hagios* in the Greek, has to do with "people separated from sin and consecrated unto God" – spirit-filled men and women who, the Bible states, spoke as they were moved by the Holy Spirit. Therefore we know that the Holy Spirit, as the third member of the Godhead, is the agent of prophecy. Remember, according to the doctrine of the Trinity, the Holy Spirit is a person, and He is God. He speaks; he can be grieved, and has many other attributes.

Let's look again at the passage, *"for prophecy never came by the will of man, but holy men of God spoke as they were moved by the Holy Spirit"* (2

Peter 1:21). The words "moved by" refer to inspiration (The Greek word for inspiration is *theopneustos*, which is made up of two composite words, "God" and "breath"). God breathed upon men and they were able to know what God was saying: their vocal organs were then used to deliver the counsel of God.

In Job 32:8, the Bible states:

> *"But there is a spirit in man, and the breath of the Almighty gives him understanding."*

So, if you are born-again, you have the Holy Spirit indwelling you, and you also have a human spirit. There is a transfer of information from the Holy Spirit to your spirit, and your spirit will make this known through your human instruments, namely your voice and brains, and in this way the word of God is transmitted.

If we look at other scriptures like 1 Corinthians 14:3, the Bible talks about the fact that *"… he who prophesies speaks edification and exhortation and comfort to men"*. Although there are different levels of prophesying, which I will get into later, at the basic level of prophesying we speak to exhort, comfort and bring the mind of God in general to the church. Our prophecy may not carry any specific revelation.

1b.   *Prophecy as forth telling or fore telling*

Prophecy can either be forth telling or fore telling. Forth telling means that prophecy can come in the form of preaching: it has to do with a simple declaration of a message from God. It may not bring any prediction and may not say anything about the future; it will just tell of things to do with the present.

During preaching, the Holy Spirit sometimes uses a human vessel to speak certain things the person has not thought of; things that are not pre-meditated. This is called Prophetic Preaching.

Sometimes men of God, especially we prophets, will teach or preach prophetically, in the sense that we may not have prepared notes beforehand. This is very peculiar to the prophetic office. Prophets study the Bible day-by-day, as a true prophet is supposed to do. They have knowledge based on the Word, and often, when they come to preach, the Holy Spirit gives their message to them.

One example of this can be taken from the Day of Pentecost, when we are told that Peter preached prophetically. How do we know this? The Bible states that many nations were represented, and those who had gathered there wondered how the disciples could speak their own languages. Some people said the believers were drunk. Immediately, Peter responded, saying that these people were not drunk, because nobody gets drunk in the morning. Instead, this was what was prophesied by Joel in Joel 2:28, that in the last days, God will pour out His Spirit upon all flesh.

From that point on, Peter began to preach, and we are told that 3,000 men were saved that day. Peter did not know beforehand that he was going to preach that sermon: it was not a message that was prepared in advance, but it was a message preached in response to people who were blaspheming the Word of God. This is what we call Prophetic Preaching, and prophets normally have this ability. Most other ministers, like teachers, will normally prepare beforehand what they are going to teach.

There is an aspect of prophecy that looks into the future. This is called "prediction". In other words, the anointing of God can come upon a vessel, especially a prophet, and he will declare events that will take place in the future. For instance, now, as an international prophet, I have a base in London where God uses me to prophesy things that are going to happen in countries and nations. Some of the things I have prophesied about include an earthquake that took place in Greece. This is documented at my church in London; I prophesied a week before the event that there was going to be an earthquake in Greece.

This is how God uses prophets. God shows them things that are going to take place: events that demonic powers had planned, to cause destruction. Prophets will prophesy about these events, and then people will take them into prayer to avert or curtail disaster. This is one of the roles of the prophet, which we will look into in greater detail later on.

I believe that the prophetic is extremely important, and that is why I want us to take the time to study this subject. Even though people in the secular world may not understand this very well, those of us who are in Christ know the power of Christ, that Jesus Christ, who is the only way and the truth and the life, was the great prophet who, though He ministered as a prophet, also ministered with all the other ministry gifts. Jesus Himself is God, and He took on flesh and became an example for us to follow. He was truly a great prophet, and now all of us are just mini-prophets who are representing Him in the earth: we are able to do the things that He did because He has given us His Spirit. He has anointed us and given us the power to represent Him.

As a prophet, when Jesus was on earth He made many predictions about events that would take place in the future. In Matthew 24, Jesus prophesied that towards the end of this world there shall be wars and rumours of wars in many places. Nation will fight against nation; kingdoms against kingdoms; there shall be earthquakes in various places, as well as destructions, famines, commotions and chaos in various parts of the world. All these things have been happening since the resurrection of Jesus, and they are increasing in intensity. We now hear of terrorist attacks in various countries; we hear of the wars of terror – so many things! Men's hearts are failing them. We hear of nuclear technology that may become a threat in the future, and so much more.

As prophets, we are called by God to prophesy, to show the events that are going to take place in the future, so that the Church can pray and intercede, either to avert disaster completely, or to minimise the fall-out that could come as a result of these events. That is why the prophetic office is so important. For me, I believe that is why God called me in 1980, and since then I have been researching and studying this subject. The reason why I stood in the prophetic office full-time eleven years ago, was to do this very thing.

My first degree in Theology was in 1998; five years later in 2003, I had finished my Masters and Doctorate degrees in Biblical Studies. At both the Masters and Doctorate levels, my research interests were in prophecy. I therefore believe that I have a lot to share by way of what God has given to me. As you know, the Bible states in John 3:27 that a man can receive nothing unless it has been given to him from heaven. So I humbly submit that everything I know came from God, by His Spirit. I do not pretend to know everything about this subject, but I do believe that what God has given to me, I can bring to you.

Chapter 2:

History of the Prophetic Movement

True prophecy started in Genesis 1:1, when God said, *"Let there be light"* (verse 3). And the Bible states, *"...there was light"* (verse 3). As we have already established, the word "prophecy" means speaking forth the mind and counsel of God. When God said, *"Let there be light"*, He was speaking by Himself and as it were, He was prophesying through His own person. I believe this was the beginning of the prophetic, which has to do with hearing God's voice and knowing God's intent through speech.

From Genesis 1 to Genesis 11, the Bible talks about the creation of the world, the fall of man, the descendants of Adam and Noah, and the periods beginning and after the flood, up to Chapter 11, which talks about the Tower of Babel and the scattering of the human race. In these chapters, the Bible talks about the generality of mankind. In Genesis 12, from verse 1 onwards, it narrows down to the Hebrew nation – the nation that came from Abraham, who was the father of Judaism and the father of the Hebrews. I hope you understand that God specifically designed and chose the Hebrew nation first. He was going to use them as a channel to bless the entire world. God was working progressively and systematically.

2a.   The origin of Hebrew prophecy

We are told in Amos 3:2, that God said to the Hebrews, *"you only have I known of all the families of the earth"*. Exodus 19:5 states the same thing, that the Hebrews are a peculiar nation.

After God, true prophecy originated with the Hebrews, the Israelites. In Genesis 20:7 for instance, the Bible talks about Abraham as a prophet. That is the first time the word "prophet" is used in the Bible. Abraham was a patriarch, a man with visions and revelations. In Genesis 15 we are told how God made a covenant with Abraham, and Abraham fell into a deep sleep, during which God cut a covenant with Abraham. This is all prophetic activity. Prophetic ministry entails visions and revelations, and hearing from God pertains to the prophetic ministry.

Also, we are told in the book of Jude that there was a man called Enoch, the seventh from Adam, who prophesied about the coming of multitudes that will come with Christ – maybe the second advent. He prophesied up to what was going to happen at the end of the world.

Through these examples, we see that prophetic activity has been going on for a very long time.

2b.   *Imitation by the heathen nations*

To prophesy means, "to speak forth". A prophet is a spokesman; one who speaks on behalf of another. Normally, therefore, the prophet is a human vessel, but in general, the one who is giving him or her the information is a deity.

For true prophecy, and in the case of the early prophecies in the Old Testament, God was the source of the prophetic inspiration. In other words, it was God who was bringing a message through the prophet, who was the vessel.

The heathen nations, those who were not the people of God, copied this. As we know, Satan has imitated everything that God has: every spiritual gift in the Bible has an imitation from the satanic kingdom. The heathen nations like the Mesopotamians, Babylonians, Canaanites and Egyptians, also had their system of prophesying. We are told in Jeremiah 23 how some prophets prophesied by Baal, a Canaanite deity.

The same applies today in African Traditional Religion. We have people prophesying by fetish means. Things have not changed. False prophets are still prophesying by false deities.

2c.   The official recognition of the prophetic office

The term, "The official recognition of the prophetic office in the Mosaic economy" refers to the time or point at which prophets were officially recognised in the Old Testament, under law during the time of Moses.

We can study this in Deuteronomy 18:9-22:

> *"When you come into the land which the LORD your God is giving you, you shall not learn to follow the abominations of those nations. There shall not be found among you anyone who makes his son or his daughter pass through the fire, or one who practices witchcraft, or a soothsayer, or one who interprets omens, or a sorcerer, or one who conjures spells, or a medium, or a spiritist, or one who calls up the dead. For all who do these things are an abomination to the LORD, and because of these abominations the LORD your God drives them out from before you. You shall be blameless before the LORD your God. For these nations which you will dispossess listened to soothsayers and diviners; but as for you, the LORD your God has not appointed such for you.*
> *The LORD your God will raise up for you a Prophet like me from your midst, from your brethren. Him you shall hear, according to all you desired of the LORD your God in Horeb in the day of the assembly, saying, 'Let me not hear again the voice of the LORD my God, nor let me see this great fire anymore, lest I die.'*
>
> *"And the LORD said to me: 'What they have spoken is good. I will raise up for them a Prophet like you from among their brethren, and will put My words in His mouth, and He shall speak to them all that I command Him. And it shall be that whoever will not hear My words,*

which He speaks in My name, I will require it of him. But the prophet who presumes to speak a word in My name, which I have not commanded him to speak, or who speaks in the name of other gods, that prophet shall die.' And if you say in your heart, 'How shall we know the word which the LORD has not spoken?'— when a prophet speaks in the name of the LORD, if the thing does not happen or come to pass, that is the thing which the LORD has not spoken; the prophet has spoken it presumptuously; you shall not be afraid of him."

In Deuteronomy 18, Moses officially recognised the priests and the Levites. Prior to this, in Chapter 17, he gave principles governing the kings. In these two chapters, Moses spelt out details about the kingly, priestly and prophetic offices, for these were the three major offices in the Old Testament under the Mosaic economy.

Chapter 18 shows that the Canaanites were involved in demonic trafficking (spiritual communication with demons), and God was very displeased with this practice. He was therefore discouraging the people of God from engaging in such trafficking of devils. His people were not to seek diviners, mediums, spiritists and such people. Instead, God was raising prophets, true vessels, true holy men of God who would speak His mind and His counsel to His people. These were the prophets.

Moses said, in Deuteronomy 18:15, *"The LORD your God will raise up for you a Prophet like me from your midst, from your brethren. Him you shall hear"*. Moses was called by God and anointed a prophet and a deliverer. He spoke the counsel of God. The Bible states in Deuteronomy 18:18, *"I will raise up for them a Prophet like you from among their brethren, and will put My words in His mouth, and He shall speak to them all that I command Him."* Here, Moses was talking about the coming of the Messiah, the Christ, who himself was a prophet from their brethren, which meant that this Messiah was going to be an Israelite. He was going to be the Great Prophet: Christ Himself coming in the likeness of men and taking on the office of the prophet, to be God's spokesman.

In Hebrews 1:1 we are told that in the Old Testament times God spoke in diverse ways and by various methods, through the prophets. But in the last days, He has chosen to speak through one Great Prophet, Jesus. And through Jesus, other prophets will also be birthed. Now we have prophets all over the world.

2d.   Old Testament prophetic ministry

From the book of Judges, we had the inauguration of the prophetic system, in the sense that Samuel stood as the leader in the beginning of a new order in the prophetic movement in the Old Testament. We are told in 1 Samuel 1 how Hannah, Samuel's mother, was barren; how she went to the Temple; how Eli the High Priest spoke with her and how God gave her a son. Hannah promised to dedicate her son to the Lord for temple service. So Samuel was raised by Eli in the temple.

The Bible states that in those days the Word of the Lord was rare. There was no widespread prophetic revelation. There had been some prophetic silence upon the earth, perhaps because of the cycle of sins of the Israelites – we see this even more in the times of the Judges. Samuel stood as the beginning of a new system of the prophetic, in the sense that he was a judge, a priest and a prophet.

1 Samuel 3:1 states:

> *"Now, the boy Samuel ministered to the Lord before Eli, and the word of the Lord was rare in those days. There was no widespread revelation."*

We are told that it came to pass at that time that when his eyes had began to go so dim that he could not see, one day while Eli was lying down before the Lamp of God went down in the Tabernacle, God called Samuel twice. Because Samuel was young (he was perhaps about twelve years old), he did not know the voice of the Lord. He ran to Eli the High Priest and twice he heard the voice saying, *"Samuel, Samuel"*. Eventually Eli told him that when he heard the voice he should say, *"Speak, LORD, for your servant hears."* Samuel did so and heard the

Word of the Lord.

As time progressed, Samuel served faithfully in the Temple under Eli, and God eventually established him as a prophet. We are told in 1 Samuel 3:19-20:

> *"Samuel grew, and the Lord was with him, and let none of his words fall to the ground. And all Israel from Dan to Beersheba knew that Samuel had been established as a prophet of the Lord."*

Samuel stood in the forefront of a new prophetic movement beginning from the book of Judges, and we are told in 1 Samuel 4:1, *"And the word of Samuel came to all Israel"*. He was recognised as a national prophet of the day. We are told that Samuel eventually established a school of prophets, where he raised other prophets. He himself went round prophesying from place to place.
1 Samuel 7:15-17 states:

> *"And Samuel judged Israel all the days of his life. He went from year to year on a circuit to Bethel, Gilgal, and Mizpah, and judged Israel in all those places. But he always returned to Ramah, for his home was there. There he judged Israel, and there he built an altar to the LORD."*

Building an altar at a place signifies a place of worship. It might interest you to know that the name of my ministry is Ramah Chapel International – I took the name from Ramah, the hometown of Samuel. The Lord told me some time ago that he called me as a Samuel to have a prophetic training centre.

Samuel went from place to place, training and raising prophets. Let me give you some more examples to help us trace the history of the prophetic movement in the Old Testament. Let's look at 1 Samuel 19:18-20:

> *"So David fled and escaped, and went to Samuel at Ramah, and told him all that Saul had done to him. And he and Samuel went and*

stayed in Naioth. Now it was told Saul, saying, "Take note, David is at Naioth in Ramah!" Then Saul sent messengers to take David. And when they saw the group of prophets prophesying, and Samuel standing as leader over them, the Spirit of God came upon the messengers of Saul, and they also prophesied."

Samuel was the leader of a prophetic company, as a prophet of prophets. He was very prominent in the Old Testament, and as a prophet, he was also an intercessor for the nation. The word *intercessor* is derived from the latin words "inter", meaning "between", and "cedere", meaning "to go". Etymologically therefore, the word *intercessor* means "a go-between". Intercessors stand in the gap for people, not just in praying for people, but even by revealing the mind and the counsel of God when ministering as a prophet. An intercessor is someone who stands between men and God; a prophet stands in for people. For instance, if I begin to prophesy to you about what is going to happen in your future, and I pray for you, I am like an intercessor.

So Samuel stood as head of a prophetic company, and that is the same ministry God has given to me, to stand as the head of a prophetic company, to raise prophets, educate people about prophecy, and teach the body of Christ about the operation of the prophetic office.

From Samuel, we are now going to talk about Elijah. In 1 Kings 17, we are told how Elijah the Tishbite appeared on the scene, giving a word about the closing of the heavens: how it would not rain. Elijah was a renowned national-level prophet. He had a contest in 1 Kings 18 with the false prophets of Baal on Mount Carmel.

1 Kings 18:20-29 states:

"So Ahab sent for all the children of Israel, and gathered the prophets together on Mount Carmel. And Elijah came to all the people, and said, "How long will you falter between two opinions? If the LORD is God, follow Him; but if Baal, follow him." But the people answered him not a word. Then Elijah said to the people, "I alone am left a prophet of the LORD; but Baal's prophets are four hundred and fifty men.

25

Therefore let them give us two bulls; and let them choose one bull for themselves, cut it in pieces, and lay it on the wood, but put no fire under it; and I will prepare the other bull, and lay it on the wood, but put no fire under it. Then you call on the name of your gods, and I will call on the name of the LORD; and the God who answers by fire, He is God." So all the people answered and said, "It is well spoken." Now Elijah said to the prophets of Baal, "Choose one bull for yourselves and prepare it first, for you are many; and call on the name of your god, but put no fire under it." So they took the bull which was given them, and they prepared it, and called on the name of Baal from morning even till noon, saying, "O Baal, hear us!" But there was no voice; no one answered. Then they leaped about the altar which they had made. And so it was, at noon, that Elijah mocked them and said, "Cry aloud, for he is a god; either he is meditating, or he is busy, or he is on a journey, or perhaps he is sleeping and must be awakened." So they cried aloud, and cut themselves, as was their custom, with knives and lances, until the blood gushed out on them. And when midday was past, they prophesied until the time of the offering of the evening sacrifice. But there was no voice; no one answered, no one paid attention."

Here, we can see that false prophets can also prophesy, but the prophets of Baal did not prophesy by Yahweh, the true God of the Israelites, who is the only God, and who created all things. They prophesied by other deities – demons, to be precise. That is why we will later look at how to distinguish whether a person is prophesying from God or from demons, or from the flesh.

1 Kings 18:29-38 continues:

"And when midday was past, they prophesied until the time of the offering of the evening sacrifice. But there was no voice; no one answered, no one paid attention. Then Elijah said to all the people, "Come near to me." So all the people came near to him. And he repaired the altar of the LORD that was broken down. And Elijah took twelve stones, according to the number of the tribes of the sons of Jacob, to whom the word of the LORD had come, saying, "Israel shall be your name." Then with the stones he built an altar in the name of the LORD; and

he made a trench around the altar large enough to hold two seahs of seed. And he put the wood in order, cut the bull in pieces, and laid it on the wood, and said, "Fill four water pots with water, and pour it on the burnt sacrifice and on the wood." Then he said, "Do it a second time," and they did it a second time; and he said, "Do it a third time," and they did it a third time. So the water ran all around the altar; and he also filled the trench with water. And it came to pass, at the time of the offering of the evening sacrifice, that Elijah the prophet came near and said, "LORD God of Abraham, Isaac, and Israel, let it be known this day that You are God in Israel and I am Your servant, and that I have done all these things at Your word. Hear me, O LORD, hear me, that this people may know that You are the LORD God, and that You have turned their hearts back to You again." Then the fire of the LORD fell and consumed the burnt sacrifice, and the wood and the stones and the dust, and it licked up the water that was in the trench."

Elijah was a *bona fide*, true, prophet. We see how he brought fire from heaven, and eventually the people returned to God. We believe that Elijah also had a school of prophets; in the sense that he had people he trained, like Elisha his servant. In 1 Kings 19:19 we are told:

"So he departed from there, and found Elisha the son of Shaphat, who was plowing with twelve yoke of oxen before him, and he was with the twelfth. Then Elijah passed by him and threw his mantle on him."

We know that Elisha was the servant of Elijah and that he inherited Elijah's mantle. We believe that Elijah may have also trained other young prophets. When we look at 2 Kings 2:1-3, we are told:

"And it came to pass, when the LORD was about to take up Elijah into heaven by a whirlwind, that Elijah went with Elisha from Gilgal. Then Elijah said to Elisha, "Stay here, please, for the LORD has sent me on to Bethel." But Elisha said, "As the LORD lives, and as your soul lives, I will not leave you!" So they went down to Bethel. Now the sons of the prophets who were at Bethel came out to Elisha, and said to him, "Do you know that the LORD will take away your master from over you today?"

27

The phrase "the sons of the prophets" implies prophets-in-training, or those belonging to a school of prophets.

The passage continues, in 2 Kings 2:5-7:

> *"Now the sons of the prophets who were at Jericho came to Elisha and said to him, "Do you know that the LORD will take away your master from over you today?" So he answered, "Yes, I know; keep silent!" Then Elijah said to him, "Stay here, please, for the LORD has sent me on to the Jordan." But he said, "As the LORD lives, and as your soul lives, I will not leave you!" So the two of them went on. And fifty men of the sons of the prophets went and stood facing them at a distance, while the two of them stood by the Jordan."*

There were sons of prophets in Bethel <u>and</u> in Jericho. We see that there were schools of prophets. The prophetic tradition was well established in the Old Testament, under Samuel, under Elijah, and as we shall soon see, under Elisha, who, after he had received the mantle from Elijah, took over the prophetic schools.

2 Kings 6:1-2 states:

> *"And the sons of the prophets said to Elisha, "See now, the place where we dwell with you is too small for us. Please, let us go to the Jordan, and let every man take a beam from there, and let us make there a place where we may dwell." So he answered, "Go.".*"

Elisha took over the schools of prophecy and began to train prophets and leaders. This movement continued, and prophetic training was well established in the Old Testament. These prophets did not write any of the books in the Bible, but eventually, we will talk about prophets who have books written in their names, like Jeremiah, Ezekiel and Daniel. Then there were the twelve minor prophets from Hosea to Malachi, each of whom was sent either to Israel in the Northern Kingdom, or to Judah in the Southern Kingdom, or both. So we had the prophetic movement up to Malachi, after which there were some four hundred years of silence during which there was no prophetic activity. At that time, the people began to complain, saying in Psalm 74:9-10:

"We do not see our signs; There is no longer any prophet; Nor is there any among us who knows how long. God, how long will the adversary reproach? Will the enemy blaspheme Your name forever?"

This marks the close of the prophetic movement in the Old Testament. In the next section, we shall look at New Testament prophetic ministry.

2e.   *New Testament prophetic ministry*

As stated above, after Malachi there was a period of silence of some four hundred years, before prophetic activity resumed in the book of Matthew, when the Messiah, who Himself was a prophet, was born. We are told about John the Baptist in Matthew 11, where it is said that of all the prophets that had been in the Old Testament, John had been the greatest. We therefore realise that John was perhaps the last prophet who completed the Old Testament period. Jesus lived in-between two testaments, in what is known as the Inter-Testamental Period. So, as far as the prophetic office is concerned, John the Baptist was the last to close the Old Testament chapter.

The New Testament period began after Jesus died and rose again. On the Day of Pentecost, prophetic activity began again in earnest. In Joel 2:28 Joel had said that in the last days God would pour out His Spirit upon all flesh; sons and daughters would prophesy; old men shall dream dreams, and young men shall see visions. This signalled the beginning of a new era: the era of the Prophetic in its fullness. Remember, in the Old Testament, the only people who had the prophetic anointing or the Holy Spirit upon them in any meaningful measure, were the prophets, the priests and the kings. But Joel promised us that in the latter days, God would pour out His Spirit upon all flesh, and this happened from the Day of Pentecost onwards.

So, right from the Day of Pentecost to the day when The Rapture shall

29

take place, prophetic activity has become common, and the Gift of Prophecy has gained particular prominence. We are told in Ephesians 3 how the Gospel was received by revelation: Paul talks about the fact that the Gospel was "revealed" to him – that implies the prophetic. Some believe that Paul may have been a prophet before becoming an apostle, given the way he received the gospel from God through the means of revelation.

In the field of Theology, there are two schools of thought on New Testament prophecy. On the one hand, there are the Cessationists (a word whose root is derived from the French word *cesser*, meaning "to stop"). The Cessationists believe that every prophetic activity, as well as the Gifts of the Spirit, stopped after the Day of Pentecost with the disappearing of the Apostles. We will soon show why this view is erroneous.

The Restorationists, on the other hand, believe in the full restoration of the prophetic, apostolic, and all the Gifts of the Spirit, which will not be taken away until the Church is taken from the earth.

Looking at this in closer detail, we realise that Ephesians 4:11 talks about ministry gifts. The Bible states that Jesus, when He ascended to heaven, gave gifts to men. We call these the five-fold ministry gifts the Headship Ministries, the Governmental Offices, or the Ascension Gifts of Christ. These are the Apostle, Prophet, Evangelist, Pastor and Teacher. The prophet's inclusion on this list shows that he or she is a church leader, just as the apostle, evangelist, pastor and teacher. We will discuss this in greater detail when we get to the Prophetic Office, but for now, it will suffice to mention that there was prophetic activity in the New Testament.

There are a number of people mentioned as prophets in the New Testament. In Acts 15:32 two men, Judas and Silas, are mentioned as prophets. In Acts 11:27-30, we are told that Agabus too was a prophet.

2f.   *Post New Testament prophetic ministry*

After the book of the New Testament was closed, we had the Post-New Testament Era. As I said earlier, Cessationists argue that there are no longer any prophets, but Ephesians 4:11-13 states:

> *"And He Himself gave some to be apostles, some prophets, some evangelists, and some pastors and teachers, for the equipping of the saints for the work of ministry, for the edifying of the body of Christ, till we all come to the unity of the faith and of the knowledge of the Son of God, to a perfect man, to the measure of the stature of the fullness of Christ."*

The key word here is "till", which speaks about a certain length of time. The question: "How long will prophets be on earth?", is answered by the Bible in Ephesians 4:13:

> *"..till we all come to the unity of the faith and of the knowledge of the Son of God..."*

What does "the unity of the faith" mean? The word "unity", from the word "unit", means "one". In other words, it refers to a time when we shall all come to one belief system: the same place of perception of spiritual truth. It appears to me that this is not going to happen on this planet. Here, there are so many churches believing different things: some even do not talk to each other! I believe we will only come to a unity of faith of the knowledge of the Son of God when we come to the fullness of the stature of Christ - when we are all raptured and are in heaven.

So prophetic ministry is very much valid even after the closure of the New Testament canon, or book. Prophetic ministry will remain valid until the Church is taken away. The prophetic movement continues, and is gaining more momentum. Currently there are many prophets in the world, on every continent: some are ministering and some are being raised. Of course, there have been many abuses and errors, but God is purging the movement, and a new breed will arise out of the old order, and Jesus shall be glorified.

Chapter 3:

Modes of Prophetic Receptivity

The word "mode", like in the French *à la mode* (i.e. fashion), means the "method" or "way". We need to look at modes of prophetic receptivity: how prophets receive words from God; how Christians hear from God; the nature of prophetic listening; and so on. God speaks in many diverse ways, but there are two primary ways in which God might speak to us – either by audio or visual means. I call this the audio and visual prophetic reception.

3a.   Audio and visual prophetic reception

"Audio" has to do with hearing. We have physical ears with which we hear in the natural. Jesus, in Revelation 2:7 says, *"He who has an ear, let him hear what the Spirit says to the churches."* I used to ask myself if the people that Jesus was talking to did not have ears, but then I realised that He was not talking about physical ears, but rather about spiritual hearing. There is a way we hear things in the natural, and there is another level of hearing things in the Spirit. Prophets hear things in the Spirit.

I, as a prophet, normally hear many things in the Spirit while I am ministering. Sometimes I can hear through the Holy Spirit, the name of somebody in the congregation, or details or facts about a person or about the future of a country. We receive prophetic messages by audio means – by hearing in the spirit realm.

We can also see into the spirit world through a gift that operates in the prophetic office and in some Christians, called the Gift of Discerning of Spirits. For instance, I believe that I was once taken into heaven, where I saw heaven in the realm of the Spirit, not in the natural. Dreams and visions also fall into this category.

3b. Dreams and visions

There are two primary ways by which we can have visual prophetic reception: through dreams and visions. The most common of these is dreams. Throughout the Old Testament, God spoke to people in dreams. People like Joseph, for instance, were very prophetic, and they received messages in dreams. In Genesis 37:9-10, we read about Joseph receiving a dream where God told him about his destiny. Joseph saw the sun, moon and eleven stars bowing down before him. Later, in the days of famine, the family of Joseph was dependent on him for survival. Joseph also interpreted Pharaoh's dream, where Pharaoh saw seven years of famine and seven years of plenty, in the form of seven thin cows and seven fat cows.

So God speaks through dreams, giving revelation to prophets, Christians in general, and even non-Christians. We know of Nebuchadnezzar, who was not of God (in the sense that he was a Babylonian, not a Jew): God spoke to him about the empires of the world that would run the course of history.

Prophets are known to have visions and revelations. Regarding visions, there are different kinds. There were several experiences in the Bible where men received prophetic messages from God through visions. We know for example, in Acts 10 about how Peter had a trance (a trance is a vision in which one's physical senses are suspended, and one becomes more conscious of spiritual realities. For instance, you may be in a room and suddenly all the windows and chairs appear to vanish and you see an angel standing in mid-air, giving you a message from God).

Some of the Old Testament prophets were called "seers", because the primary way they received their messages was through visions and dreams.

Also in the Old Testament, when we talk about a prophet using the Hebrew word *nabi*, we would most likely be talking about a prophet who speaks on the spur of the moment by hearing in the Spirit and speaking forth, bubbling like a fountain the message he has received from God. We will learn more about this when we get to the Tools of the Prophetic Office.

3c.   *Prophetic similitudes*

Let's now look at prophetic similitudes, or prophetic symbolisms. It is not every time that a prophet will receive a message from God in plain language: many times a prophet will receive information that is coded. Often, when a prophet is ministering in a crowd, he might see certain symbolic images: we call these similitudes. It is then up to the person receiving the prophetic word to decode the message. Sometimes the prophet will also have the ability to interpret what he sees.

Hosea 12:10 states,

> *"I have also spoken by the prophets, and have multiplied visions; I have given symbols through the witness of the prophets."*

Prophets often speak in symbolic language. In fact, there is a close relationship between the prophetic and the apocalyptic. The biblical apocalyptic is a field of prophetic activity where symbols are used, like in the books of Revelation and Daniel. Daniel is an example of a visionary prophet or a seer. In Daniel 1:17 onwards, we are told that he had understanding of all kinds of dreams and visions. He was the one who interpreted the dreams of Nebuchadnezzar; he himself had a lot of visions about the ram and the goat, the four different beasts representing the four world empires, and so on. These were all symbolic.

The angel who was showing him interpreted all of the things that Daniel saw. Symbolic revelation always has to be interpreted, in order for the recipient to understand. The Bible states that it is the glory of God to conceal a matter, and it is the glory of kings to search it out (Proverbs 25:2).

We find this phenomenon of prophetic symbolism also mentioned in Numbers 12:6-8. Miriam, Moses' sister, had spoken against Moses. God was angry, and He brought Miriam and Aaron to the Tent of Meeting. He spoke to them:

> *"Then He said,"Hear now My words: If there is a prophet among you, I, the LORD, make Myself known to him in a vision; I speak to him in a dream. Not so with My servant Moses; He is faithful in all My house. I speak with him face to face, Even plainly, and not in dark sayings; And he sees the form of the LORD. Why then were you not afraid to speak against My servant Moses?"*

The phrase "dark sayings" (some versions say "dark speeches") refers to symbolisms, that is, a way that God will communicate through the prophet in symbolic speech or imagery. But Moses had a high-level prophetic office, in the sense that God spoke to him face-to-face.

3d.   Supernatural messengers

The prophetic message may come through supernatural messengers, for example, in Luke, when Zacharias and Elizabeth were praying for a child. An angel, a supernatural messenger, not a normal flesh-and-bone living being, was sent to them. We are told in Luke 1:10-13:

> *"And the whole multitude of the people was praying outside at the hour of incense. Then an angel of the Lord appeared to him, standing on the right side of the altar of incense. And when Zacharias saw him, he was troubled, and fear fell upon him.But the angel said to him, "Do not be*

afraid, Zacharias, for your prayer is heard; and your wife Elizabeth will bear you a son, and you shall call his name John."

This prophetic message, delivered through the appearance of an angel, is a type of open vision. Zacharias saw the angel by seeing into the spirit world.

Similarly, in Daniel 10:10-14 we read:

"Suddenly, a hand touched me, which made me tremble on my knees and on the palms of my hands. And he said to me, "O Daniel, man greatly beloved, understand the words that I speak to you, and stand upright, for I have now been sent to you." While he was speaking this word to me, I stood trembling. Then he said to me, "Do not fear, Daniel, for from the first day that you set your heart to understand, and to humble yourself before your God, your words were heard; and I have come because of your words. But the prince of the kingdom of Persia withstood me twenty-one days; and behold, Michael, one of the chief princes, came to help me, for I had been left alone there with the kings of Persia. Now I have come to make you understand what will happen to your people in the latter days, for the vision refers to many days yet to come."

3e.   "Rhema" out of "Logos"

Another way that God might deliver prophetic messages is through what is called "Rhema out of Logos". *Rhema* is a Greek word that means "the spoken Word". *Logos* means "the written Word". There are times when you are reading the Bible; you suddenly find the portion of the scripture that you are reading becomes alive to you, as if it jumps out of the Bible to you. This means that God is speaking to you, and what He is saying to you is related to the part of scripture that has been highlighted in this way.

Once, before God called me to the ministry, I was reading a part of Chronicles, and I got to the part that says, *"My sons do not be negligent, for the Lord God has chosen you to minister before him"* (2 Chronicles

29:11). I was literally arrested by that portion of scripture: it was a confirmation of my call, as before then, a lot of men of God had prophesied to me that God was going to use me mightily.

3f.   *Prophetic utterances*

God frequently speaks through prophetic utterances. In other words, a person is used by God to speak out a prophetic message to you. For instance, many times I call people and speak to them things I never thought of, things initiated by the Holy Spirit. Sometimes what I say comes to pass dramatically, because the messages originated from God. If they had originated from me, they wouldn't come to pass! I have prophesied about nations and people in messages delivered through my voice.

In this book, we will be looking a lot at prophetic utterances, because this is a major area of prophetic ministry.

3g.   *Christophany*

Although Jesus is in heaven, there are times He chooses to reveal himself. There are many prophets, and especially apostles, who have seen the risen Christ, and have been given messages from him. An example can be found in Acts 23:11:

> *"But the following night the Lord stood by him and said, "Be of good cheer, Paul; for as you have testified for me in Jerusalem, so you must also bear witness at Rome."*

The Lord stood by Paul. This was a visible appearance of Christ, to Paul - a Christophany.

Another example of a visible manifestation of Christ can be found in Revelation 1:1-17:

"The Revelation of Jesus Christ, which God gave Him to show His servants—things which must shortly take place. And He sent and signified it by His angel to His servant John, who bore witness to the word of God, and to the testimony of Jesus Christ, to all things that he saw. Blessed is he who reads and those who hear the words of this prophecy, and keep those things which are written in it; for the time is near.

John, to the seven churches which are in Asia: Grace to you and peace from Him who is and who was and who is to come, and from the seven Spirits who are before His throne, and from Jesus Christ, the faithful witness, the firstborn from the dead, and the ruler over the kings of the earth.

To Him who loved us and washed us from our sins in His own blood, and has made us kings and priests to His God and Father, to Him be glory and dominion forever and ever. Amen.

Behold, He is coming with clouds, and every eye will see Him, even they who pierced Him. And all the tribes of the earth will mourn because of Him. Even so, Amen.
I am the Alpha and the Omega, the Beginning and the End," says the Lord, "who is and who was and who is to come, the Almighty.""

Chapter 4:

Different Levels of Prophetic Activity

I wrote earlier that in Joel 2:28, the famous Old Testament prophet prophesied that in the last days God would pour out His Spirit upon all flesh. He told us that sons and daughters will prophesy, old men shall dream dreams, and young men will have visions. In other words, there was going to be an accelerated prophetic activity in the body of Christ, in contrast to the Old Testament, where there were only a few people who were privileged to have the indwelling of the Holy Spirit.

This means that every one who is a *bona fide* Christian, who has the Holy Spirit in him or her, has some kind of prophetic potential. But we also notice that the prophetic potential of individuals vary from person to person. It is like a swimming pool, which starts from the shallow end and gradually, becomes deeper and deeper, until one gets to the deepest part. So it is among Christians – there are different levels of prophetic activity.

4a. Prophetic sensing, perceptions, or impressions

We can talk about prophetic sensing, prophetic perceptions, or prophetic impressions. Prophetic sensing has to do with Christians picking up something in the Spirit, especially after praying. When that happens, you know that something is wrong somewhere, but you cannot tell precisely what that is. Sometimes you might go to a house, and the moment you step into it, you know there is something evil in that house, but you cannot pinpoint where it is coming from, or what is causing it.

To give an example from the scriptures, sometimes you can sense that you must not undertake a journey you had planned to undertake, because there will be disaster. Let's look at Acts 27:9-13:

"Now when much time had been spent, and sailing was now dangerous because the Fast was already over, Paul advised them, saying, "Men, I perceive that this voyage will end with disaster and much loss, not only of the cargo and ship, but also our lives." Nevertheless the centurion was more persuaded by the helmsman and the owner of the ship than by the things spoken by Paul. And because the harbour was not suitable to winter in, the majority advised to set sail from there also, if by any means they could reach Phoenix, a harbour of Crete opening toward the southwest and northwest, and winter there .

When the south wind blew softly, supposing that they had obtained their desire, putting out to sea, they sailed close by Crete. But not long after, a tempestuous head wind arose, called Euroclydon."

Here, Paul was among a group of prisoners going to Rome to stand trial before the emperor. Before the ship set sail, he made a profound statement, saying that he sensed that there was going to be a problem with the ship. He could not tell exactly where or how it would take place, but he knew that there was going to be a disaster. That is prophetic sensing.

4b.   The Spirit of Prophecy

The Spirit of Prophecy is the transfer of prophetic inspiration by induction, due to the richness of the prophetic atmosphere. Here, a person without the capacity to prophesy ordinarily receives this ability due to the prophetic presence.

This describes the situation where a person who is not particularly prophetic goes into a meeting that is highly charged prophetically, or into a worship service where the prophetic anointing is strong, or happens to be around a prophet who has a very strong prophetic anointing, and this person starts to prophesy.

Interestingly, I have found a good analogy with electrical engineering; in fact, I realise that some of the principles in electricity are similar to those in prophetic activity. For example, in electrical engineering, there is something called magnetism. A strong magnet on a table emanates invisible rays, known as magnetic flux, which constitutes a magnetic field, the density of which will depend on the strength of the magnet.

If you put a piece of iron metal in the presence of this magnet, it will become magnetised. In other words, it will eventually behave like a magnet. There are some other metals which, when put in the presence of this strong magnet, will catch the magnetic flux and behave like a magnet as long as the magnet is nearby. But when the strong magnet is removed, these metals will eventually lose that magnetic force which they have received. This is called magnetic induction.

Sometimes a person who hangs around a prophet or comes into a place with a strong prophetic presence (or "prophetic flux"), may find himself or herself beginning to prophesy. But when that prophetic presence is removed, he or she ceases to prophesy.

For example, in 1 Samuel 10:9-12, we see what happened when Saul met the prophet Samuel and was told that he was going to become king:

> "So it was, when he had turned his back to go from Samuel, that God gave him another heart; and all those signs came to pass that day. When they came there to the hill, there was a group of prophets to meet him; then the Spirit of God came upon him, and he prophesied among them. And it happened, when all who knew him formerly saw that he indeed prophesied among the prophets, that the people said to one another, "What is this that has come upon the son of Kish? Is Saul also among the prophets?" Then a man from there answered and said, "But who is their father?" Therefore it became a proverb: "Is Saul also among the prophets?"

The interesting thing here is that Saul was not a prophet. But because he came into the midst of a prophetic company, a group of people with a strong prophetic presence, he had what I term "prophetic induction". A prophetic anointing was induced in him, and he also prophesied, to the surprise of others who had hitherto not known him to be a prophet.

In 1 Samuel 19:19-24 we read:

> *"Now it was told Saul, saying, "Take note, David is at Naioth in Ramah!" Then Saul sent messengers to take David. And when they saw the group of prophets prophesying, and Samuel standing as leader over them, the Spirit of God came upon the messengers of Saul, and they also prophesied. And when Saul was told, he sent other messengers, and they prophesied likewise. Then Saul sent messengers again the third time, and they prophesied also. Then he also went to Ramah, and came to the great well that is at Sechu. So he asked, and said, "Where are Samuel and David?" And someone said, "Indeed they are at Naioth in Ramah." So he went there to Naioth in Ramah. Then the Spirit of God was upon him also, and he went on and prophesied until he came to Naioth in Ramah. And he also stripped off his clothes and prophesied before Samuel in like manner, and lay down naked all that day and all that night. Therefore they say, "Is Saul also among the prophets?"*

Here was Saul, who had murder in his heart, and was looking for David to kill. He was told that David had gone to the prophet Samuel in his hometown Ramah, where Samuel had his school of prophets, his prophetic company. We are told that when Saul got there and came into the presence of the prophets, he also prophesied… he had another prophetic induction! This was a man with a murderous heart who came into a strong prophetic atmosphere. Instead of carrying out his evil plan, he joined the prophets. His outer tunic was taken off, and he lay down and prophesied. The atmosphere was so rich in prophetic activity that Saul could not help but join in.

Sometimes, if you hang around a prophet many times and you serve the prophet, there may be a transfer of the prophetic anointing. We know about Elisha: how he served and poured water on the hands of

Elijah. Of course, Elisha was destined to become a prophet, but the Bible states that as he served Elijah, Elisha eventually received a double portion of the prophetic anointing.

The prophetic anointing is easily transferable; it is one grace that can easily rub upon other people when they are around a prophet, in a prophetic medium, or in an atmosphere that is rich in prophetic intensity.

4c.   The Gift of Prophecy

This is one of the nine Gifts of the Spirit listed in 1 Corinthians 12. Its purpose is to edify, exhort and comfort the saints. It is inspirational. 1 Corinthians 14:1-3 states:

> *"Pursue love, and desire spiritual gifts, but especially that you may prophesy. For he who speaks in a tongue does not speak to men but to God, for no one understands him; however, in the spirit he speaks mysteries. But he who prophesies speaks edification and exhortation and comfort to men."*

"To edify" means "to build up". I am sure you know the English words "edifice", "castle", "fortress" and "stronghold". When you have a car whose battery runs down, and you charge the battery, you can be said to be edifying the battery. The Bible states that prophetic activity in the midst of the Church makes the Church stronger. In fact, the Bible states that he who prophesies edifies the Church and makes the Church stronger. How does this happen?

A person who has the Gift of Prophecy will need a Word base – he or she will need to read the scriptures a lot, because when inspiration comes upon him or her, the Holy Spirit will utilise the words of God that are in him or her, to bring out words that can strengthen people.

Sometimes Christians may be discouraged; prophecy rings out and they become encouraged. Remember, when somebody gives a prophecy, it is not he or she who premeditates what he or she is going to say. There is a prophetic flow right from the Holy Spirit through his or her spirit, and this comes to edify the Church. So edification is very important.

Exhortation comes from a Greek root, *kerusso*, which means "to preach", or "to proclaim". In the same vein, a person who prophesies can be used by God to give His people certain words of admonishment, counsel or advice.

1 Corinthians 14 also speaks about comfort. Sometimes people are bereaved, feeling down, and wanting to give up on life because things are getting tough, and these people need God's comfort. From time to time, the Holy Spirit comforts us (He is even called "the comforter", or *parakletos* in the Greek).

The Bible states that Jesus said that we would have tribulations in this world (Matthew 24:9). The word "tribulation" is from the Greek word *thlipsis*, which basically has to do with pressure of any sort. There are so many pressures in this life: pressures in marriage, in raising children, in trying to put one's financial life together, and so on. Jesus comes to comfort us, and many times He uses the medium of prophecy, speaking words of comfort directly to us.

This is very important. We need more people with the Gift of Prophecy to prophesy in the Church, so that the people of God can be strengthened.

1 Corinthians 12:10 states:

> *"To another the working of miracles, to another prophecy, to another discerning of spirits, to another different kinds of tongues, to another the interpretation of tongues."*

You see that not everyone has the Gift of Prophecy in the Church, but some people have been endowed with this supernatural ability, and it is important that we take note of them, help them develop their gift, and encourage them to come out when under inspiration in an assembly, and give words of edification, exhortation and comfort.

There is something I want to mention here about prophecy. As I said earlier, prophecy depends on a person's spiritual level of maturity; it depends on how much Word you have inside you, because normally the Holy Spirit will do a scan on your spirit and pick up scriptures that would suit a particular occasion.

If you look at Romans 12:6, you will see what the Bible states about this:

> *"Having then gifts differing according to the grace that is given to us, let us use them: if prophecy, let us prophesy in proportion to our faith."*

The phrase "in proportion to our faith" means that we cannot prophesy beyond the measure of our faith. In other words, somebody who just got born again today - if he or she has the gift of prophecy - may not prophesy for more than five minutes, because he or she would not have enough words in his or her spirit. But the person who has been in the faith for a long time, like myself, who has been born-again since 1980, would have a solid Word base – I have studied the Bible for a long time; I used to read several chapters of the Bible every day, so I have enough Word base inside me, and by the grace of God I can prophesy for long time without stopping, if the Holy Spirit so comes upon me. I would have enough things to say by the Spirit, because when the Sprit searches my spirit, He would find so much Word or knowledge to use to encourage people.

So the level at which a person with the Gift of Prophecy will prophesy will depend on the Word level that the person has.

4d. Prophetic presbytery

The word "presbytery" is from a Greek word *presbuteros*, which means an elder. The plural *presbuteroi* means elders, a group of men of God, or a group of pastors. Prophetic presbytery is the coming together of a group of elders, to speak into the life of an individual. It is effectively the harnessing of the prophetic potential of the group, giving vent to prophetic proclamation by one or more members of the unit. Normally we see this in ordination ceremonies, when someone is being released into pastoral ministry or service, or into any ministry for that matter.

What happens is that a group of pastors or men of God come together (it is desirable that at least one of them should be a prophet), and join together their prophetic potentials. It is much like in electricity, where we have what we call a series circuit. When you put many batteries together in a series, you have a total of all the battery voltages. If you put three 1.5-volt batteries together in a series, you will have a total of 4.5 volts – this is more powerful than a single battery.

A prophetic presbytery can be a very powerful unit. When the elders come together and they all lay hands on a young minister or any individual, a prophetic potential is established, and one of them can act as a spokesperson for the unit, prophesying accurately the counsel of God.

There is an example of prophetic presbytery in 1 Timothy 4:14:

> *"Do not neglect the gift that is in you, which was given to you by prophecy with the laying on of the hands of the eldership."*

Paul is saying here to Timothy to remember that when he was about to be ordained, Paul and other elders laid hands on him. Paul is urging Timothy to remember the prophecy given concerning his life, future and ministry. Paul is also encouraging Timothy to begin acting on that prophecy. When prophets lay hands on people, gifts that are dormant can be activated – that is one aspect of the prophetic office. The anointing of the prophet has the ability to stir people up to service and to use their gifts that have been lying dormant.

4e.   *The prophetic office*

There is a difference between the Gift of Prophecy and the prophetic office. The prophetic office is the highest level of the prophetic. For instance, I am a prophet; I stand in an office. There are many people who call themselves prophets, but they are not yet mature and sound in doctrine and wisdom, to be able to stand in the prophetic office. They do not have what it takes. They may have the gift to make proclamations, even with revelation gifts operating in their lives, but that does not mean that they are ready for the office.

Here is one example: in 1 Corinthians 1:7, Paul was writing about the Corinthian Church, a Church that he planted. A lot of spiritual activity was taking place in Corinth: that is why 1 Corinthians Chapter 12 talks about the Gifts of the Spirit, and Chapter 14 talks about prophecy and tongues. We see that there was a lot of charismatic activity. In fact, this may have been the most charismatic church in the first century.

But Paul went on in 1 Corinthians 3:1, to say some things that almost seem contradictory. He said that he could not consider the Corinthians as spiritual people (the Greek word here is *pneumatikos*), but as babies, because he fed them with milk and not with solid food. Even up to the time of Paul's writing, they were not ready for solid food. This means that there were certain revelations of scripture, certain deep things of God that they did not understand, because they were not yet well established or skilled in the Word of righteousness.

Paul said in 1 Corinthians 13:11, *"When I was a child, I spoke as a child, I understood as a child, I thought as a child. But when I became a man, I put away childish things."* So it is with the things of the Spirit. There are spiritual babies, spiritual children and spiritual men. To grow in Christ is dependent on knowledge. In 1 Peter 2:2, the Bible states, *"As newborn babes, desire the pure milk of the word, that you may grow thereby"*.

So you see, having spiritual gifts does not mean a man is mature. This is what many people do not understand in the Church today. They think that if a man can raise the dead and prophesy accurately, then he must be a great man of God: he must really be mature. No, no, no!

We are told about the Church of Corinth that they had <u>all</u> the spiritual gifts, but yet they were babies: they had not studied, been trained or equipped, and they had not come to maturity. One of the reasons why Paul could not consider them as spiritual people, but as babies, is that there was strife and division among them. People who are not spiritually mature are always quarrelling. Paul said that they were behaving like mere men, as if they had not been saved. These are all signs of immaturity.

God cannot put a man in an office who is immature, and who is not knowledgeable in Christ. We will look at this in greater detail when we discuss the prophetic office later. But let me first define who is a prophet. My definition is:

> **The individual, who has first a divine calling into that particular office, and through training and service, has been established in that leadership position. He carries a far stronger prophetic mantle than one who just operates in the Gift of Prophecy.**

Let's look at sections of this definition in greater detail:

i. *"...a divine calling into that particular office, and through training and service..."*

A person who is a prophet must first have been called by God to become a prophet. There are three phases in a prophet's life: the call, the preparation and the commission. I have seen many people, who presume to be prophets, but they only had the call, and they moved from the call and tried to commission themselves. They called themselves prophets and did not wait for the training; they were not prepared. Tragically, this ends in disaster.

ii. *"...has been established in that leadership position."*

A prophet is a leader, just like the apostles, evangelists, pastors and teachers. You cannot put a novice into the ministry; you cannot put into the ministry somebody who doesn't know how many books there are in the Bible, or who, when asked, "Where is Haggai?" responds, "In the New Testament". Such a person cannot be put into an office, because he cannot handle the Word of God properly. He cannot educate people with sound doctrine; he himself needs to be educated. That helps us to know who is a prophet and who is not.

iii. *"…carries a far stronger prophetic mantle than one who just operates in the Gift of Prophecy."*

It is not he who says he is a prophet; it is he whom God says is a prophet. Prophets must conform to the standard set in the Bible. Many Christians are confused: some are following very young people who claim to be prophets, but are not yet mature: they cannot handle the Word of God properly; they themselves need to be taught. They can neither be leaders nor prophets. The prophet carries a stronger prophetic mantle beyond the ordinary. They have greater authority in the spirit realm.

1 Samuel 3:19-20 states:

> *"So Samuel grew, and the LORD was with him and let none of his words fall to the ground. And all Israel from Dan to Beersheba knew that Samuel had been established as a prophet of the LORD."*

When a person comes to maturity, the body of Christ – especially the leaders of the Church – will know who is a prophet and who is not. When you stand before them to minister, they can tell whether you are mature or not. Here we are told, *"Samuel grew"*, which means that he started as a child, as a boy in the temple, serving Eli the High Priest.

Samuel was very loyal. Today, there are many young ones who have the Gift of Prophecy, but do not want to serve anybody. Once they have the gift, they disobey their head pastor. They rebel, and go off to try to start their own ministry. They cannot go far because they are not mature or ready. That is why anyone called to the office of the prophet

51

should be fed and taught until mature, and only then should they be released into the prophetic office.

"...Samuel grew, and the Lord was with him, and let none of his words fall to the ground" (1 Samuel 3:19). This means that everything Samuel said came to pass. He knew how to discern the voice of God. Some immature prophets do not know how to discern the voice of God: they speak from their own hearts; and sometimes they are even influenced by demons, and then they speak things that bring chaos and sadness among people. They do not even know how to use wisdom to package the word that they have received. All this comes with maturity.

As in the field of marketing, products that are well packaged attract more buyers than those that are poorly packaged. All this comes with wisdom in the prophetic office.

Ephesians 4:11 states:

> *"And He Himself gave some to be apostles, some prophets, some evangelists, and some pastors and teachers, for the equipping of the saints for the work of ministry, for the edifying of the body of Christ."*

The people who operate in the five-fold ministry gifts are the Church leadership, including the prophet. They equip and train the saints by teaching and preaching; they have what it takes to teach and educate people; and they are sound enough in doctrine to impart knowledge. If you cannot do that, then you are not qualified to be a prophet. You had better go and sit down and learn, and wait until the right time, when God Himself will set you in the prophetic office.

We have some examples in the New Testament, of people whom the Bible calls prophets. In other words, the Holy Spirit acknowledged their prophetic office. See what Acts 11:27 states:

> *"And in these days prophets came from Jerusalem to Antioch."*

Here, the word "prophets" (*prophetai* in the Greek) is in the plural.

There were many who were recognised as prophets in the New Testament, though not all of them were mentioned by name.

Acts 11:28 continues:

> *"Then one of them, named Agabus, stood up and showed by the Spirit that there was going to be a great famine throughout all the world, which also happened in the days of Claudius Caesar. Then the disciples, each according to his ability, determined to send relief to the brethren dwelling in Judea. This they also did, and sent it to the elders by the hands of Barnabas and Saul."*

Agabus was a prominent prophet of the New Testament. Though the others were not mentioned by name, they had the status of New Testament prophets, and I believe they were recognised by God.

Let's look at the last example in this section, Acts 13:1-3:

> *"Now in the church that was at Antioch there were certain prophets and teachers: Barnabas, Simeon who was called Niger, Lucius of Cyrene, Manaen who had been brought up with Herod the tetrarch, and Saul. As they ministered to the Lord and fasted, the Holy Spirit said, "Now separate to Me Barnabas and Saul for the work to which I have called them." Then, having fasted and prayed, and laid hands on them, they sent them away."*

Again here in the Church at Antioch (also called the Antiochan Church) five people are mentioned as prophets and teachers. In other words, some of them may have been prophets, some teachers, or they were all both prophets and teachers. A person can stand in more than one office. For instance, I am a prophet and a teacher, and the Lord has been speaking to me recently about moving into an apostolic office.

The prophets in the New Testament were mature men. I believe that Saul (who was later called Paul) was a prophet and a teacher, and later on became an apostle.

Chapter 5:

The Nature and Character of the Prophetic Word

The words that we prophets speak under the inspiration of the Holy Spirit are called The Prophetic Word. This is a Word from God.

The parable of the sower is found in three passages in the synoptic gospels; it can be found it Mark 4, Matthew 13 and Luke 8. The version in Luke 8 makes a very profound statement in verse 11b: *"The seed is the word of God."* Once you get a prophecy, it is like a seed you have sown in the ground, and you have to cultivate that Word. We will look at this further, as we go along.

5a.   Conditional and unconditional prophecy

Prophecy may be conditional or unconditional, especially when a prophecy looks into or predicts the future. Usually, personal prophecies given to individuals and even to nations are conditional. In a few instances, prophecies may be unconditional, but there is often a part we must play to bring our prophecies to pass.

This has caused much confusion in the body of Christ today. You hear somebody say, "The prophet gave me a prophecy that in two years' time I would travel to America, but it's been five years, and I'm still in Ghana!" Sometimes what transpires is that the prophet gave a true word from the Lord, but as with any prophecy received, the recipient has a part to play to bring it to pass.

For instance, if I gave you a word by the Spirit, that in three years' time you will be a man of God, you would have to do certain things to be a man of God, like reading the Bible daily, studying deeply, praying a lot, fasting and so on. But if you do not fast, do not pray, and do not read the Bible during those three years, how would you become a man of God in that time? The requirements would have not been met. That is why some prophecies are conditional.

Here is another example: if God says you will be the first in your examination at secondary school, and you do not study, how would that prophecy come to pass? God works with us to bring to pass what He Himself has said.

In 1 Timothy 1:18-19, Paul writes to Timothy, saying:

"This charge I commit to you, son Timothy, according to the prophecies previously made concerning you, that by them you may wage the good warfare, having faith and a good conscience, which some having rejected, concerning the faith have suffered shipwreck".

There is a very interesting application here about prophecy. Paul is reminding Timothy about some prophecies given to him. There were some things that God expected Timothy to do to bring those prophecies to pass, but Timothy had done nothing about them. Paul mentions three interesting things when it comes to the fulfilment of prophecy. The first thing he states is, *"...that by them you may wage the good warfare"*. What does the word "them" stand for? This is what we call in Theology "the antecedent". "Them" stands for the prophecies themselves, which means that one needs prophecy itself, to fight a good warfare to bring the prophecy to pass. But why does one have to fight spiritually?

I once thought to myself, "A fight is not a good thing: if you meet people fighting on the street, it doesn't seem like a good thing". But God is saying here that fighting in the spiritual realm is a good thing. Remember, we have enemies, and these are not human beings. The Bible states we wrestle not against flesh and blood, but against principalities, powers, and the rulers of the darkness of this age and against spiritual hosts of wickedness (fallen angels) (Ephesians 6:12).

The people we think are our enemies in the flesh are not our real enemies: our real enemies are spirit beings, demons, and powers of darkness.

In 1 Corinthians 16:9 Paul states, *"For a great and effective door has opened to me, and there are many adversaries."* A great door here means an opportunity for the Gospel, and for Paul's life and ministry. God has many things prepared for us. We are told in 1 Corinthians 2:9-10:

> *"Eye has not seen, nor ear heard, nor have entered into the heart of man the things which God has prepared for those who love Him. But God has revealed them to us through His Spirit. For the Spirit searches all things, yes, the deep things of GOD."*

We see here that God is a good God. That is why we say that God is good all the time; He is full of goodness and has good plans for us. He states, *"For I know the thoughts that I think toward you…, thoughts of peace and not of evil, to give you a future and a hope."* (Jeremiah 29:11). God is always planning and thinking good things about us.

On the other hand, our archenemy Satan is also thinking up evil plans to destroy us. We are told in John 10:10 that Jesus said, *"The thief does not come except to steal, and to kill, and to destroy. I have come that they may have life, and that they may have it more abundantly."*

The Bible states in 2 Corinthians 10:3-4, *"For though we walk in the flesh, we do not war according to the flesh. For the weapons of our warfare are not carnal but mighty in God for pulling down strongholds."* It therefore means that a Christian is on the spiritual battlefield. In other words, demons, who are our enemies, try to stop our promises from coming to pass. They hear the prophecies and they themselves go to try to hinder them.

Remember, the great Apostle Paul, in 1 Thessalonians 2:17-18 said:

> *"But we, brethren, having been taken away from you for a short time in*

presence, not in heart, endeavoured more eagerly to see your face with great desire. Therefore we wanted to come to you—even I, Paul, time and again—but Satan hindered us."

Sometimes the supernatural forces of darkness hinder us. They hinder our preaching; they try to hinder our marriages; they try to hinder even our understanding of the Bible; they don't want us to progress spiritually; and they don't want us to come to our prophetic destiny. So we must fight.

In order for our prophecies to come to pass, we have to pray daily, fast, and wage spiritual warfare. There is a difference between prayer and spiritual warfare, although the two are connected: they are like twins. When we pray, we make requests and petitions before the Father. We also go to God for wisdom, strength and power. But then, after we have got the power, what next? We must now confront the demons. God is not going to confront the demons for us.

When you get a prophecy, the demons will seek to thwart, hinder, and nullify it, to make sure that it does not come to pass. So you have to wrestle with them. Ephesians 6:10-20 states:

"Finally, my brethren, be strong in the Lord and in the power of His might. Put on the whole armor of God, that you may be able to stand against the wiles of the devil. For we do not wrestle against flesh and blood, but against principalities, against powers, against the rulers of the darkness of this age, against spiritual hosts of wickedness in the heavenly places. Therefore take up the whole armor of God, that you may be able to withstand in the evil day, and having done all, to stand. Stand therefore, having girded your waist with truth, having put on the breastplate of righteousness and having shod your feet with the preparation of the gospel of peace; above all, taking the shield of faith with which you will be able to quench all the fiery darts of the wicked one. And take the helmet of salvation, and the sword of the Spirit, which is the word of God; praying always with all prayer and supplication in the Spirit, being watchful to this end with all perseverance and supplication for all the saints— and for me, that utterance may be given

to me, that I may open my mouth boldly to make known the mystery of the gospel, for which I am an ambassador in chains; that in it I may speak boldly, as I ought to speak."

The Greek word used in this passage, for the wiles or the plans of the devil, is *methodea*, which refers to the methodology or strategy of the devil. He has a strategy for all of us, to try to destroy us. But thank God for the sake of Christ, who says we cannot be defeated. We shall be victorious.

So to summarise, when you receive a prophecy, you can be sure that the enemy will come against you. That is why you must wage a *good* warfare. Now why is this warfare good? It is good because after you have prevailed, you can inherit your inheritance, possess your possessions, and take hold of that which God has destined for your life.

The next thing Paul states in 1 Timothy 1:18-19, is that we must have faith. Once while I was preaching, the Lord told me that if I spoke under the prophetic inspiration and the people do not believe Him, then it is as if they would be saying that He was a liar. Imagine, someone thinking that God is a liar! The Bible states in Romans 3:4, *"Indeed, let God be true but every man a liar"*. God is always true. Anything that God is supposed to have said that has not come to pass even though all the conditions were met probably was not from God. Whatever God says comes to pass. He is the Spirit of Truth.

So as you can imagine, we need faith. Without faith, many things would go wrong in our Christian lives. Indeed, faith was the very channel by which we became saved. Ephesians 2:8 states, *"For by grace you have been saved through faith, and that not of yourselves; it is the gift of God"*. Throughout the Christian life, we need faith even to operate spiritual gifts, to operate the prophetic office, and for everything. We must trust God and believe His Word.

If you have a prophecy and you do not believe it, then it will fall to the ground. No wonder in 2 Chronicles 20:20, the Bible states:

"So they rose early in the morning and went out into the Wilderness of Tekoa; and as they went out, Jehoshaphat stood and said, "Hear me, O Judah and you inhabitants of Jerusalem: Believe in the LORD your God, and you shall be established; believe His prophets, and you shall prosper."

Assuming the prophets are speaking the mind of God, you have to believe the word, or nothing will happen. Even in prayer, if you pray for something, and you don't believe God will do it, then I'm afraid God cannot do it.

The next thing Paul talks about in 1 Timothy 1:18-19, is "a good conscience". Conscience is part of the spirit of man. There are three parts to the physical body: there is the outer part of the body, the middle part of the body, and the inner part of the body.

In biology, we talk about the exoderm and the endoderm, and we also talk about the skin, the somatic cells. Then we come inside to the musculoskeletal system, which is the muscles and so on, followed by the internal organs. And then, when it comes to the soul, we have three parts: the mind or the understanding, the will or the decision-making centre, and the emotions.

We also have three parts of the spirit: first, the intuition (the part that has premonition and is able to know things without having the facts); second, the contact line, which is the part of the spirit that communicates with God. Adam and Eve had their contact line before they fell; after the fall their contact lines were cut off. All those who are not born-again Christians have their contact lines disconnected, with the possibility of being connected once they give their lives to Jesus.

The third and last part of the human spirit is the conscience. This is also called "the moral umpire". Its function is to tell us if we are doing wrong. In the Dispensation of Conscience, during the time of Adam and Eve, there was no Bible, but Adam and Eve could tell when they sinned; their conscience told them that what they had done was wrong. Even when the unsaved do bad things, they know that they are doing wrong. But because they are under the dominion and power of sin, they cannot help but sin.

A good conscience has to do with righteousness: walking right with God. That means that if you receive a prophecy (which is just a picture, so to speak, showing what God's intent is for us) but you are not walking in righteousness, then most probably your prophecy will not come to pass. I know that because when you are living in sin, you cannot exercise faith, since sin brings a gap between you and God. We are told in Galatians 5:6 that *"For in Christ Jesus neither circumcision nor uncircumcision avails anything, but faith working through love".* In the New Testament, love is how to live for God; to walk right with God. Faith does not work without love; it does not work when you are not walking right with God.

I can give you even more proof. One thing that I wrote about earlier was good warfare. Demons are very interesting: if you are not obeying God, you cannot command demons to obey you, since demons are rebels, and if you also become a rebel, that puts you on the same level as them. Since you cannot command them to go, your prophecy will be hindered.

For instance, we are told in 2 Corinthians 10:3-5:

> *"For though we walk in the flesh, we do not war according to the flesh. For the weapons of our warfare are not carnal but mighty in God for pulling down strongholds, casting down arguments and every high thing that exalts itself against the knowledge of God, bringing every thought into captivity to the obedience of Christ..."*

Verse 6 states, *"...and being ready to punish all disobedience when your obedience is fulfilled".* How can you drive away disobedient demons when you yourself are in disobedience to God? Rather, you are on their side.

In that respect, prophecy has conditions before it can come to pass. Let me give you one more example. Let's look at Jeremiah 18:7-10:

> *"The instant I speak concerning a nation and concerning a kingdom, to pluck up, to pull down, and to destroy it, if that nation against whom I have spoken turns from its evil, I will relent of the disaster that I thought to bring upon it. And the instant I speak concerning a nation and concerning a kingdom, to build and to plant it, if it does evil in My sight so that it does not obey My voice, then I will relent concerning the good with which I said I would benefit it."*

God is saying, "If I declare judgment on a nation that is sinning, and if that nation responds by repenting and confessing their sins, then the prophecy of doom that I gave through the prophet will not be carried out." Even prophecies for nations depend on those nations: they are not automatic. Do not think, "The prophet said that in the next two years I will be a millionaire", and then you do not work hard but rather just lie in bed… dear friend, it will not come to pass. Prophecy is conditional.

From Jeremiah 29:11, I am going to give you a wonderful biblical example about how a prophecy was given, and what the people did to bring it to pass. I have already said that you have to pray, fast and wage war, to bring a prophecy to pass.

Jeremiah 29:11-14 states:

> *"For I know the thoughts that I think toward you, says the LORD, thoughts of peace and not of evil, to give you a future and a hope. Then you will call upon Me and go and pray to Me, and I will listen to you. And you will seek Me and find Me, when you search for Me with all your heart. I will be found by you, says the LORD, and I will bring you back from your captivity; I will gather you from all the nations and from all the places where I have driven you, says the LORD, and I will bring you to the place from which I cause you to be carried away captive."*

Let's see what Jeremiah actually said about the captivity. In Jeremiah 25:11, Jeremiah prophesied to the people of Judah because they had gone so much into sin and idol worship. God was angry, and the prophets had warned them that they would be carried away captive to

Babylon. The northern kingdom, which was known as Samaria or Israel, had been taken to Assyria, and God was warning His people through Jeremiah. See what Jeremiah said in Jeremiah 25:11:

> *"And this whole land shall be a desolation and an astonishment, and these nations shall serve the king of Babylon seventy years. 'Then it will come to pass, when seventy years are completed, that I will punish the king of Babylon and that nation, the land of the Chaldeans, for their iniquity,' says the LORD; 'and I will make it a perpetual desolation."*

So Jeremiah prophesied that the people of God would go into captivity for seventy years, after which time they would be released from captivity. Now something interesting happened: many, many years later – possibly hundreds of years later, another prophet read what had been written, and took it up. Let's go to Daniel 9:1-3:

Now look at what Daniel said:

> *"In the first year of Darius the son of Ahasuerus, of the lineage of the Medes, who was made king over the realm of the Chaldeans— in the first year of his reign I, Daniel, understood by the books the number of the years specified by the word of the LORD through Jeremiah the prophet, that He would accomplish seventy years in the desolations of Jerusalem.*
> *Then I set my face toward the Lord God to make request by prayer and supplications, with fasting, sackcloth, and ashes."*

Daniel didn't just say, "Well, it's been seventy years now; let's wait and see what will happen – we shall just come out of captivity." It was not going to happen automatically. Daniel understood that even though God had said it, if they didn't pray and wage war with the demons they had to contend with – the people would not be able to come out of captivity.

Remember, whenever somebody is held in spiritual bondage, there are demons involved, and those demons must be wrestled with. That is why a drunkard who has done everything to change, but cannot

63

change, must wrestle with the demon of alcohol by which he has been bound. Until he wrestles with and defeats that demon, he will not be able to stop drinking.

We have heard people say, "This New Year I will make a resolution: no more smoking: I will throw away all my cigarettes!" Just wait three weeks: before you know it, the person is smoking again. The reason is that the demon who is holding him down has not yet been dealt with. That is why we have to wrestle with and defeat demons, through the power that is in the blood of Jesus, and through the Word of God, by the power of the Holy Spirit.

The Bible states in Daniel 9:3-5:

> *"Then I set my face toward the Lord God to make request by prayer and supplications, with fasting, sackcloth, and ashes. And I prayed to the LORD my God, and made confession, and said, "O Lord, great and awesome God, who keeps His covenant and mercy with those who love Him, and with those who keep His commandments, we have sinned and committed iniquity, we have done wickedly and rebelled, even by departing from Your precepts and Your judgments."*

Daniel began to confess sins, and many things happened. Let's see what happened behind the scenes in the Spirit. Daniel 10:1-13 states:

> *"In the third year of Cyrus king of Persia a message was revealed to Daniel, whose name was called Belteshazzar. The message was true, but the appointed time was long; and he understood the message, and had understanding of the vision. In those days I, Daniel, was mourning three full weeks. I ate no pleasant food, no meat or wine came into my mouth, nor did I anoint myself at all, till three whole weeks were fulfilled. Now on the twenty-fourth day of the first month, as I was by the side of the great river, that is, the Tigris, I lifted my eyes and looked, and behold, a certain man clothed in linen, whose waist was girded with gold of Uphaz! His body was like beryl, his face like the appearance of lightning, his eyes like torches of fire, his arms and feet like burnished bronze in colour, and the sound of his words like the voice of a multitude. And I,*

Daniel, alone saw the vision, for the men who were with me did not see the vision; but a great terror fell upon them, so that they fled to hide themselves. Therefore I was left alone when I saw this great vision, and no strength remained in me; for my vigour was turned to frailty in me, and I retained no strength. Yet I heard the sound of his words; and while I heard the sound of his words I was in a deep sleep on my face, with my face to the ground.

Suddenly, a hand touched me, which made me tremble on my knees and on the palms of my hands. And he said to me, "O Daniel, man greatly beloved, understand the words that I speak to you, and stand upright, for I have now been sent to you." While he was speaking this word to me, I stood trembling. Then he said to me, "Do not fear, Daniel, for from the first day that you set your heart to understand, and to humble yourself before your God, your words were heard; and I have come because of your words. But the prince of the kingdom of Persia withstood me twenty-one days; and behold, Michael, one of the chief princes, came to help me, for I had been left alone there with the kings of Persia."

Daniel fasted for 21 days, standing in the gap, interceding and waging war, so that a prophecy that had been given hundreds of years earlier would be fulfilled. An angel appeared to tell him that on his way, bringing the answer to the problem of the Jews who had been taken captive to Babylon, the angel had been resisted, until Michael - the archangel in charge of God's army (the army commander or general) had come to his rescue. So Daniel succeeded: the angel broke through because Daniel continued to fast and wage war.

Anything that happens in the spiritual world eventually happens in the physical world, which meant that because Daniel prevailed spiritually, the people of God could be rescued physically. This applies to every area of our lives, where anything we are facing is spiritual. Once the spiritual problem is dealt with in the spirit world, then we will see everything resolved in the natural.

Let me give you an example. There is a text in Ezra that tells us what happened to Daniel's people. I believe that Daniel's warfare and prayer provoked a release. Ezra 1:1-3 states:

Now in the first year of Cyrus king of Persia, that the word of the LORD by the mouth of Jeremiah might be fulfilled, the LORD stirred up the spirit of Cyrus king of Persia, so that he made a proclamation throughout all his kingdom, and also put it in writing, saying,
Thus says Cyrus king of Persia:
All the kingdoms of the earth the LORD God of heaven has given me. And He has commanded me to build Him a house at Jerusalem which is in Judah. 3 Who is among you of all His people? May his God be with him, and let him go up to Jerusalem which is in Judah, and build the house of the LORD God of Israel (He is God), which is in Jerusalem."

Daniel's spiritual warfare brought about some physical results. We see that Cyrus, the King of Persia, was not a believer, so to speak. He was not a Jew. So then, how come he suddenly put out a decree that the people of Israel should leave - go out of captivity and rebuild their country? This could only be God's work. It was because someone read a prophecy, prayed and waged war, and after prevailing in the spirit world, events began to happen in the natural.

This is always true. Sometimes you have financial problems, and unless you break through in the Spirit, you cannot be prosperous in the natural.

There are so many other examples: for instance, in the book of Jonah, we are told that Jonah was sent by God to a place called Nineveh to preach against the very wicked Assyrians. Jonah went, and let's see what happened. Jonah 1:1-3:10 states:

"Now the word of the LORD came to Jonah the son of Amittai, saying, "Arise, go to Nineveh, that great city, and cry out against it; for their wickedness has come up before Me." But Jonah arose to flee to Tarshish from the presence of the LORD. He went down to Joppa, and found a ship going to Tarshish; so he paid the fare, and went down into it, to go with them to Tarshish from the presence of the LORD. But the LORD sent out a great wind on the sea, and there was a mighty tempest on the sea, so that the ship was about to be broken up.

Then the mariners were afraid; and every man cried out to his god, and threw the cargo that was in the ship into the sea, to lighten the load. But Jonah had gone down into the lowest parts of the ship, had lain down, and was fast asleep. So the captain came to him, and said to him, "What do you mean, sleeper? Arise, call on your God; perhaps your God will consider us, so that we may not perish." And they said to one another, "Come, let us cast lots, that we may know for whose cause this trouble has come upon us." So they cast lots, and the lot fell on Jonah. Then they said to him, "Please tell us! For whose cause is this trouble upon us? What is your occupation? And where do you come from? What is your country? And of what people are you?" So he said to them, "I am a Hebrew; and I fear the LORD, the God of heaven, who made the sea and the dry land."

Then the men were exceedingly afraid, and said to him, Why have you done this?" For the men knew that he fled from the presence of the LORD, because he had told them. Then they said to him, "What shall we do to you that the sea may be calm for us?"—for the sea was growing more tempestuous. And he said to them, "Pick me up and throw me into the sea; then the sea will become calm for you. For I know that this great tempest is because of me." Nevertheless the men rowed hard to return to land, but they could not, for the sea continued to grow more tempestuous against them. Therefore they cried out to the LORD and said, "We pray, O LORD, please do not let us perish for this man's life, and do not charge us with innocent blood; for You, O LORD, have done as it pleased You." So they picked up Jonah and threw him into the sea, and the sea ceased from its raging. Then the men feared the LORD exceedingly, and offered a sacrifice to the LORD and took vows.

Now the LORD had prepared a great fish to swallow Jonah. And Jonah was in the belly of the fish three days and three nights.

Chapter 2

Then Jonah prayed to the LORD his God from the fish's belly. And he said: " I cried out to the LORD because of my affliction, And He answered me. "Out of the belly of Sheol I cried, And You heard my voice. For You cast me into the deep, Into the heart of the seas, And the floods surrounded me; All Your billows and Your waves passed over me. Then I said, 'I have been cast out of Your sight; Yet I will look again toward Your holy temple. The waters surrounded me, even to my soul; The deep closed around me; Weeds were wrapped around my head. I went down to the moorings of the mountains; The earth with its bars closed behind me forever; Yet You have brought up my life from the pit, O LORD, my God. " When my soul fainted within me, I remembered the LORD; And my prayer went up to You, Into Your holy temple. " Those who regard worthless idols Forsake their own Mercy. But I will sacrifice to You With the voice of thanksgiving; I will pay what I have vowed. Salvation is of the LORD."

So the LORD spoke to the fish, and it vomited Jonah onto dry land.

Chapter 3
Now the word of the LORD came to Jonah the second time, saying, "Arise, go to Nineveh, that great city, and preach to it the message that I tell you." So Jonah arose and went to Nineveh, according to the word of the LORD. Now Nineveh was an exceedingly great city, a three-day journey in extent. And Jonah began to enter the city on the first day's walk. Then he cried out and said, "Yet forty days, and Nineveh shall be overthrown!" So the people of Nineveh believed God, proclaimed a fast, and put on sackcloth, from the greatest to the least of them. Then word came to the king of Nineveh; and he arose from his throne and laid aside his robe, covered himself with sackcloth and sat in ashes. And he caused it to be proclaimed and published throughout Nineveh by the decree of the king and his nobles, saying,
Let neither man nor beast, herd nor flock, taste anything; do not let them eat, or drink water. But let man and beast be covered with sackcloth, and cry mightily to God; yes, let every one turn from his evil way and from the violence that is in his hands. Who can tell if God will turn and relent, and turn away from His fierce anger, so that we may not perish? Then God saw their works, that they turned from their evil way; and God relented from the disaster that He had said He would bring upon them, and He did not do it."

This confirms what we read earlier in Jeremiah 18:7:

"The instant I speak concerning a nation and concerning a kingdom, to pluck up, to pull down, and to destroy it, if that nation against whom I have spoken turns from its evil, I will relent of the disaster that I thought to bring upon it."

Jonah went to Nineveh to proclaim judgment because of the sin of the Assyrians, who were very wicked people. This is exactly what happened to the Israelites: God gave them so many promises, for instance, about how He would bless them and bring them to Canaan – a land flowing with milk and honey. But because of their sins, many of them could not enter Canaan. It is not that the prophecy was not true, but that the prophecy was <u>conditional</u>. The people had to obey God.

In the case of Nineveh, the same thing happened. When Jonah went to Nineveh, he even gave a date when the people were going to be destroyed: in 40 days judgment would strike. The people repented. Jonah 3:10 states,

"Then God saw their works, that they turned from their evil way; and God relented from the disaster that He had said He would bring upon them, and He did not do it."

God doesn't want to judge people, but He is forced to do it because He is holy. His nature is such that He cannot tolerate sin. He is forced to bring punishment. Due to His great love, His punishment is redemptive. He punishes you so that when you feel the pain, you can come running back to Him. He is a good God!

There are some unconditional prophecies, those words that God has given to a prophet, that do not need man to fulfil them. These have to do with God's own prophetic agenda for the Church and for nations. Here, the ultimate plan of God will be fulfilled, whether we pray or not.

Revelation 21:7 says:

"He who overcomes shall inherit all things, and I will be his God and he shall be my son."

This is a general prophecy about those who overcome. God promised that they would inherit all things. This prophecy will surely come to pass, because there will surely be people who will obey God and be overcomers.

There is another piece of scripture I would like us to look at. Revelation 1:7-8 states:

> "Behold, He is coming with clouds, and every eye will see Him, even they who pierced Him. And all the tribes of the earth will mourn because of Him. Even so, Amen. "I am the Alpha and the Omega, the Beginning and the End," says the Lord, "who is and who was and who is to come, the Almighty."

This is a prophecy about Jesus' second coming, the advent. In Theology we call it the *parousia*. *Parousia* was a Greek word used for the visit of a prominent high-ranking official. The word refers to the visit of a high-ranking official whose coming is to remain – it is permanent. Imagine a king who has come to a town, and is going to remain there, with those particular townspeople.

We are told that He is coming with the clouds. The Bible states that every body living in the world at that time will see Jesus coming with the clouds, including the Jews, the people who pierced Him. We are also told in John 1:1:

> "In the beginning was the Word, and the Word was with God, and the Word was God. He was in the beginning with God. All things were made through Him, and without Him nothing was made that was made. In Him was life, and the life was the light of men. And the light shines in the darkness, and the darkness did not comprehend it.
> There was a man sent from God, whose name was John. This man came for a witness, to bear witness of the Light, that all through him might believe. He was not that Light, but was sent to bear witness of that Light. That was the true Light which gives light to every man coming into the world. He was in the world, and the world was made through Him, and the world did not know Him. He came to His own, and His

70

own did not receive Him. But as many as received Him, to them He gave the right to become children of God, to those who believe in His name."

And in Matthew 24:30:

"Then the sign of the Son of Man will appear in heaven, and then all the tribes of the earth will mourn, and they will see the Son of Man coming on the clouds of heaven with power and great glory."

This is an unconditional prophecy; whether you fast and pray, or beg God, it doesn't matter Christ <u>will</u> *come* back. It is certain, and will surely come to pass.

Another example of unconditional prophecy can be found in Revelation 21:1-8:

"Now I saw a new heaven and a new earth, for the first heaven and the first earth had passed away. Also there was no more sea. Then I, John, saw the holy city, New Jerusalem, coming down out of heaven from God, prepared as a bride adorned for her husband. And I heard a loud voice from heaven saying, "Behold, the tabernacle of God is with men, and He will dwell with them, and they shall be His people. God Himself will be with them and be their God. And God will wipe away every tear from their eyes; there shall be no more death, nor sorrow, nor crying. There shall be no more pain, for the former things have passed away." Then He who sat on the throne said, "Behold, I make all things new." And He said to me, "Write, for these words are true and faithful." And He said to me, "It is done! I am the Alpha and the Omega, the Beginning and the End. I will give of the fountain of the water of life freely to him who thirsts. He who overcomes shall inherit all things, and I will be his God and he shall be My son. But the cowardly, unbelieving, abominable, murderers, sexually immoral, sorcerers, idolaters, and all liars shall have their part in the lake which burns with fire and brimstone, which is the second death."

This is a prophecy about the new heaven and the new earth. This earth, we are told, will pass away – it will be burnt by fire, as we are told in 2 Peter 3:10. After God destroys this earth, He will create a new earth and a new heaven. That is an unconditional prophecy – whether we pray or not, it will happen.

5b.   *Prophecy is partial*

To see what it means to say that prophecy is partial, let's look at 1 Corinthians 13:9-11. Paul writes:

> *"For we know in part and we prophesy in part. But when that which is perfect has come, then that which is in part will be done away. When I was a child, I spoke as a child, I understood as a child, I thought as a child; but when I became a man, I put away childish things."*

Paul writes, *"…we prophesy in part."*, which means that however good a prophecy sounds, it is not the whole picture. It's like a piece of a jigsaw puzzle. You must not dwell on a part of the whole; you must sometimes <u>wait</u> for the whole picture. That is why you cannot build your life on prophecies; you must build your life on the Word of God. Prophecy is just a guide or a light in the time of difficulty; it gives you clues, so that you can continue the race and finish well.

This is why in churches based on prophecy with little or no teaching, the people go astray and sometimes they may not even end up in heaven. I am a prophet and I cherish prophecy immensely, and even though I have prophesied dramatic things sometimes very accurately, I still know that as good as prophecy is, it is always in part. Let me give you an example to buttress this point.

There was a time when a woman came to me for prophetic counselling, and I told her that I saw she was going to marry a Sunday school teacher. She was then a single medical doctor, and she was very excited to hear the prophecy. I later heard that she was transferred to another part of the country, but before she moved, another prophet

72

also told her that her next-door neighbour would become her husband. Some time after she took up her new post, she started courting the gentleman who lived next door. Later in their relationship she discovered that her suitor was also a Sunday school teacher. They eventually got married! What I said to her was one part; the other prophet also saw another part.

5c.   *Prophecy is progressive*

We talk about "progressive revelation", which means that sometimes a prophecy comes to you, and since it is in part, you will need another part, at a later time, to enable you to progress towards the whole picture. That's why it becomes progressive: there is a movement of prophetic revelation.

I see a transition from Old Testament revelation to New Testament revelation: in the Old Testament, many prophecies were given whose fullness was only seen in the New Testament. Even the prophets in the Old Testament did not understand some of the things they were prophesying, because those prophecies had to continue into the New Testament before we could understand them fully. To give you an example, let's look at 1 Peter 1:10-12:

> *"Of this salvation the prophets have inquired and searched carefully, who prophesied of the grace that would come to you, searching what, or what manner of time, the Spirit of Christ who was in them was indicating when He testified beforehand the sufferings of Christ and the glories that would follow. To them it was revealed that, not to themselves, but to us they were ministering the things which now have been reported to you through those who have preached the gospel to you by the Holy Spirit sent from heaven—things which angels desire to look into."*

What Peter is saying here is that the prophets of the Old Testament, like Isaiah, Malachi, Micah, Amos, Jonah, Obadiah, Jeremiah, Ezekiel and others, spoke about the Messiah. But they themselves did not understand a lot of things that they said, because prophecy is progressive. The prophetic picture has now progressed to the extent that we are getting the full picture.

The Old Testament prophets were told that they should not worry about the fact that they did not understand, because it was not to themselves they were prophesying. They were prophesying about those who were to obtain grace, *"...the prophets who prophesied of the grace that would come to you"* (1 Peter 1:10b).

Some of the Old Testament prophets said that the Messiah would be a king. Others said that he would be a servant. How can a king also be a servant? At the time, this was incomprehensible, because the revelation had not progressed far enough. But in the fullness of time, we can now see the whole picture. Jesus is a servant king.

Remember, in the body of Christ, we do not do things like those of the world. In the world, how can a minister be your servant? In actual fact, the word "minister" (*diakonos* in the Greek) means "a servant". But how many ministers would come to your house and wash your feet? Jesus washed the feet of His own disciples (see John 13). Scripture declares that he who will be greatest among us shall be least. Christ was the most humble person on earth, and through His ministry he became great. Humility is supposed to be a defining characteristic of Christians everywhere.

Sometimes when I prophesy, I may tell the congregation that I hear a name, like Michael, for example. Two men may stand up both called Michael. Then another revelation may come to me by the Holy Spirit – "the one who has three sisters", for instance. After I say that, one of the Michaels will sit down, and the other one would remain. I would ask the one standing how many sisters he has, and he would say "three".

Why didn't God just give all the information at once? He doesn't do that. Sometimes He says one thing, to see how the people respond. If they respond and come forward, the next revelation will proceed.

74

That's how prophecy is progressive.

5d. *Prophecy is creative*

There is supernatural energy in the prophetic word. When God spoke out and prophesied by Himself, as it were, in Genesis 1:3, He said, *"Let there be light"*. And there was light. God spoke the World into being.

Hebrews goes a step further to report on the same. In Hebrews 11:1-3 we read:

> *"Now faith is the substance of things hoped for, the evidence of things not seen. For by it the elders obtained a good testimony. By faith we understand that the worlds were framed by the word of God, so that the things which are seen were not made of things which are visible."*

We cannot understand the creation of the world by logic or reason. These worlds were made (The Greek word *Katartizo* is used here: it means to "arrange", "set in order", "equip", "complete", "make fully ready" and "prepare") by the Word of God, by prophecy. There is a Hebrew word, *Bara*, which means "to make something out of nothing". God made the world out of nothing. This we can only understand by faith.

Bara explains the power of the prophetic word. It implies that the Word of God can be creative. That is why a prophet can sometimes look into a person's eyes and speak a new womb into a lady who previously had no womb.

5e. *Prophecy is powerful*

Prophecy has energy and power. Every prophetic word coming from a prophet under the anointing is very powerful: it carries supernatural energy.

In Jeremiah 1:9-10, we see:

> *"Then the LORD put forth His hand and touched my mouth, and the LORD said to me: "Behold, I have put My words in your mouth. See, I have this day set you over the nations and over the kingdoms, To root out and to pull down, To destroy and to throw down, To build and to plant."*

This is the commission of Jeremiah as a prophet. The Bible states, *"...the Lord put forth his hand"* (Jeremiah 1:9). This is a metaphor, a figure of speech. It is called an anthropomorphic statement. The word "anthropomorphic" is of Greek origin: it is made up of two words: *anthropos*, which is the Greek word for "man", and *morphe*, which means "form".

Because God is a spirit, we only describe Him in human terms because we have nothing else to describe him with. So for instance, when the Bible states *"the eyes of God"* (see 2 Chronicles 16:9), do not think that God has got eyes like you and I. Neither has God got hands like our hands. Solomon says that God fills the heavens and the earth (1 Kings 8:27). Of course, we only see God in Jesus in bodily form, but that is another matter. We are talking about the fact that *"... the Lord put forth his hand and touched my mouth..."* (Jeremiah 1:9). That is an anthropomorphic statement.

The hand of the Lord is symbolic. It stands for the power of God. This means that the power of the prophetic was transferred to Jeremiah, such that Jeremiah received a prophetic anointing from that day forward. The Bible states in Jeremiah 1: 9-10, *"Behold, I have put my words in your mouth. See, I have on this day..."*. That God said He had set Jeremiah over the nations and over the kingdoms, to root out and to pull down, means that Jeremiah, by his prophesying, would bring judgement upon nations. He would build nations and he would

76

sit as a prophet over nations and decree things that would happen to nations, just by speaking. That is how powerful the prophetic word is.

Chapter 6:

The Management of Prophecy

6a.   Recording the prophetic word

Every prophecy you receive must be recorded. Do you know why? Let me give you an example to illustrate why: normally when a president is giving a speech, there are many microphones in front of him or her; these microphones come from media houses – everyone wants to hear what the president is saying, because a president is an important personality. But when God is speaking through a prophet, we often don't record the message, because we don't realise that the message is from God Himself.

In Luke 1:67-70, we are told that God spoke by His prophets. It is God who is doing the speaking; He is only using the voice of the prophet. So when the prophet is speaking under the prophetic anointing, remember, it is God who is speaking.

As a prophet, I have prophesied things before where the people did not listen, and the end result was death. Once, during a Sunday meeting, I saw a white car in a vision, number plate and all. The Lord told me to announce that there was a lady there whose fiancé owned that car, and that the man was going to travel to Kumasi, a city in Ghana, on the coming Tuesday, and that he would not come back alive. When I prophesied this, the lady came forward. All the descriptions I gave were accurate, and the lady confirmed that her fiancé was indeed planning to drive to Kumasi on Tuesday. If the prophecy had not made him cancel his trip, he would not have returned home alive.

This is certainly not a man speaking! How could I have known about this in the future? I am only a mortal man. In fact, once God showed me the day a person was going to die, for various reasons. God showed me on a Sunday, that the person was going to die on Tuesday. And it happened exactly on Tuesday. How could I have known this?

This is what we call prophetic prediction. God knows everything from the end to the beginning. Because we must wage war with our prophecies, and because we must handle them well to bring them to pass, we <u>must</u> first record them.

I want to show you something in Revelation 1:1, but first let me explain the difference between revelation and prophecy, though the two have something in common. Sometimes we combine these two terms, and for that we have the term "prophetic revelation". Prophecy means speaking forth the mind of God, but how will the Word of God come to us? Like we saw earlier, sometimes one can receive a revelation, which is the unveiling of a mystery (*apokalupto* in the Greek). It means that there is something about you, which another person does not know, but the Holy Spirit reveals it to that other person. I can meet a lady and say, "You have a boy as your first born". I did not know that; the boy has been around for a while, but it had not been unveiled to me – God had to open my eyes to see it.

A revelation can be written down but not spoken. But when the revelation is spoken, it becomes prophecy. We call that prophetic revelation.

Revelation 1:1-3 states:

> *"The Revelation of Jesus Christ, which God gave Him to show His servants—things which must shortly take place. And He sent and signified it by His angel to His servant John, who bore witness to the word of God, and to the testimony of Jesus Christ, to all things that he saw. Blessed is he who reads and those who hear the words of this prophecy, and keep those things which are written in it; for the time is near."*

We first see that this revelation originated from God the Father, and it was given to Jesus Christ. It is like a letter sent from one country to another. When someone posts a letter from say, London to South Africa, the letter will first go through the London postal system. Here it will pass from one officer to another, and yet another! In the South African postal system, the letter will also move from person to person before the local postman will deliver the letter to the recipient's door. This is how a revelation can be passed from location to location in the Spirit until it appears in the natural world.

Let's trace the path of the revelation in the Book of Revelation. It was passed from God to Jesus Christ, to show to his servant John the Apostle. Jesus passed the information on to an angel, who passed it on to John, who passed it on to the seven churches in Asia Minor. When the information came, what did the apostle say? Revelation 1:3 states:

> *"Blessed is he who reads and those who hear the words of this prophecy, and keep those things which are written in it; for the time is near."*

In a way, there is one word missing here. As I stated earlier, when you get a prophecy, the first thing to do is to record it. Write it down, or tape it. Since this is the Word of God, you need to analyse it. In fact, educational psychologists tell us that we need to hear a message seven times, before it actually registers. So sometimes when you think you have heard the preaching, you have not really heard it. Many times after I finish preaching, I stand at the door of our church and say, "Tell me two scriptures I quoted." Most people would have forgotten.

You need to have a hard copy. You must record every prophecy, since it concerns your life. A prophecy can be about your future; it can be a life-or-death situation. You must analyse it and know how to wage war.

Let's look again at *"Blessed is he who reads..."* (Revelation 1:3). The reason why I say that there is a word missing is because you cannot read something that is not written. So, in applying this verse to our lives when managing prophecy, I would phrase it thus:

"Blessed it he who first writes a prophecy, and then reads the prophecy over and over again, and hears it over and over, until they begin to understand the prophecy in the Spirit; and keep it or act it out."

6b. *Prophetic witness*

Prophetic witness is about testing prophecy, and this will be addressed later in greater detail. But here is a summary. Prophetic witness means that when we receive a prophecy, our spirit must bear witness with the prophecy. For instance, we must bear witness to the prophetic word by the application of the written word and prayer. A prophecy might be a new revelation, or a confirmation of a previous prophecy. Sometimes prophets see things never before perceived by the recipient of the prophecy. If that happens, the person receiving the prophecy must validate the word before taking action. There are several examples in the Bible, such as the call of Elisha, David and Paul, among others.

Prophecy may be submitted to church leadership or eldership for validation. What this means is that when you get a prophecy, you must have a witness in your spirit. Don't just accept anything anybody says, and go and do it. You must first check it out.

6c. *Times and seasons*

God works with times and seasons for our lives – He works with His own calendar. Sometimes you need to know the proper timing of prophetic events, so that you do not go ahead of God. You need to walk in step with Christ. There are some things, which you know now through prophecy, but it may be that the time to take action is not now. Be careful: many have made grave mistakes. Young pastors have dreamt that they were preaching to 5,000 people, and they thought it would happen in the next month, but it could be twenty years away. They left their schooling to go into pastoral ministry and became failures, because it was not the proper time to take action. When you do something for God at the wrong time, it will never bear fruit. Instead, it will become counter-productive.

There are two Greek words used for time. The word *Chronos* refers to the quantity of time, for example, thirty days or one year. There is another Greek word, *Kairos*. This tells you what particular events are happening within *Chronos*. If *Chronos* says thirty days, the question is, what are the special events happening within those thirty days? For instance, if within April, we had Easter celebrations, *Chronos* can tell us that there are thirty days in April, but *Kairos* will say that in April there are important days like Good Friday and Easter Sunday.

God has divided our lives into *Kairoi*; that is, the times and seasons that we have been talking about. Let's look at Daniel 10:1, for instance:

> *"In the third year of Cyrus king of Persia a message was revealed to Daniel, whose name was called Belteshazzar. The message was true, but the appointed time was long..."*

The word for "appointed time" is the Greek word *Kairos*. In other words, God has determined a particular time for different things in our lives like overseas travel, marriage and ministry. God told me about six years ago that my international ministry would begin in 2006, the year I would turn 46. He said that in 2006 I would go to America and hold a very big conference, after which my international ministry would be launched and I would begin to go to nations.

This happened in February 2006, when I held a conference in America, which was attended by bishops, ministers and others. Since then, my ministry has been transformed. If I hadn't waited for the six years to be up; if I had moved sooner or delayed, things would not have worked, because it would not have been the appointed time.

In 1 Chronicles 12:32, we are told about the sons of Issachar. The

Bible states that the sons of Issachar were men of understanding: they were men who knew what Israel ought to do, and when to do it. They knew the times and the seasons. We as Christians must also know the times and seasons that God has determined for us, because things work best in the timing of God.

There is provision in the timing of God. In fact, in Psalm 102:13, God said that He would arise to have favour upon Zion, for the appointed time for favour had come: the season of God had come for Israel to be favoured.

Let me give you an example about Moses, from Acts 7:17-36:

> *"But when the time of the promise drew near which God had sworn to Abraham, the people grew and multiplied in Egypt till another king arose who did not know Joseph. This man dealt treacherously with our people, and oppressed our forefathers, making them expose their babies, so that they might not live. At this time Moses was born, and was well pleasing to God; and he was brought up in his father's house for three months. But when he was set out, Pharaoh's daughter took him away and brought him up as her own son. And Moses was learned in all the wisdom of the Egyptians, and was mighty in words and deeds. 'Now when he was forty years old, it came into his heart to visit his brethren, the children of Israel. And seeing one of them suffer wrong, he defended and avenged him who was oppressed, and struck down the Egyptian. For he supposed that his brethren would have understood that God would deliver them by his hand, but they did not understand. And the next day he appeared to two of them as they were fighting, and tried to reconcile them, saying, 'Men, you are brethren; why do you wrong one another?' But he who did his neighbor wrong pushed him away, saying, 'Who made you a ruler and a judge over us? Do you want to kill me as you did the Egyptian yesterday?' Then, at this saying, Moses fled and became a dweller in the land of Midian, where he had two sons. ''And when forty years had passed, an Angel of the Lord appeared to him in a flame of fire in a bush, in the wilderness of Mount Sinai. When Moses saw it, he marveled at the sight; and as he drew near to observe, the voice of the Lord came to him, saying, 'I am the God of your fathers—the*

84

God of Abraham, the God of Isaac, and the God of Jacob.' And Moses trembled and dared not look. Then the LORD said to him, "Take your sandals off your feet, for the place where you stand is holy ground. I have surely seen the oppression of My people who are in Egypt; I have heard their groaning and have come down to deliver them. And now come, I will send you to Egypt." "This Moses whom they rejected, saying, 'Who made you a ruler and a judge?' is the one God sent to be a ruler and a deliverer by the hand of the Angel who appeared to him in the bush. He brought them out, after he had shown wonders and signs in the land of Egypt, and in the Red Sea, and in the wilderness forty years."

We are told that when Moses was forty years, it came into his heart that he was a deliverer. He knew his life's purpose. But the time was not yet. He tried to implement his calling as a deliverer, and made a tragic mistake because he did not understand the times and seasons. Because it was not his time, even his own people did not receive him as a deliverer. We are told that he went to Midian, and he trained and served in the wilderness as a shepherd for another forty years, before the final appointed time, or the *kairos*, the time of favour, came.

So it will be with your own life. If you are called to be a businessman, there is a time when you will become wealthy. If you are called to be a man of God, there is a time when God will bring you out. Don't come out before your own time! You will be miserable; you will have problems; you may go astray; and you can fall into a trap, because there will be no grace or protection for you. Moses was almost killed because there was no covenant between him and God at the time.

Habakkuk also said the same thing. In Habakkuk 2:1-3, the Bible states that Habakkuk stood upon the wall, to hear what the Lord would say. Eventually he made a profound statement about vision. He said the Lord said:

"Write the vision and make it plain on tablets, that he may run who reads it. For the vision is yet for an appointed time; but at the end it will speak, and it will not lie..."

85

This means that the things which God has spoken to you; the things you have seen in dreams – they may not be meant for now. You saw yourself preaching in a whole stadium; you are a young man: it could happen thirty years from now! What you must do is to continue to prepare. Don't resign from your job just yet – you may end up being destitute. God will not help you in this, because He has not sent you. Your time has not come.

6d. Three phases of the prophetic word

A prophetic word may have three phases, as follows: revelation, interpretation and application. The revelation is the raw prophetic word spoken. The prophetic word is often spoken with imagery: it is usually symbolic. As stated above, many times prophets see symbolic things in visions: for example, a vision of a child may not refer to a baby; it may refer to a new church. The prophet must be mature to be able to interpret prophetic symbolism or imagery.

Likewise, you as a Christian must learn the Bible very well, so that you also can interpret imagery, for God often uses symbols from the Bible. Many young prophets, because they are immature and do not know the Bible very well, can have revelation as a raw material, but they cannot interpret what they are seeing. Wrong interpretation leads to wrong application, and so many people have been led astray in this way.

Daniel was noted for prophetic symbolism. We call his book apocalyptic, or biblical apocalyptic. The book of Revelation is also an apocalyptic book: it uses a lot of symbols and imagery, like "the seven trumpets" (Revelation 8:6), "a locust with a tail" (Revelation 9:1-12), and "a dragon with a tail that swept away one-third of the stars" (Revelation 12:4). One has to find out what each of these images means. The tail of the dragon stands for the power of the dragon, as the power of the dragon is located in its tail. This speaks of the power of Satan in persuading or deceiving one-third of the angels in heaven, to commit rebellion against the Almighty God (Revelation12:4).

If you read the book of Daniel, you will see that Daniel had a lot of dreams. For instance, he dreamt in Daniel 8 about the ram and the male goat, which was referring to the conflict between the Kingdom of Greece and the Medo-persian Empire.

Daniel 8:1-6 states:

> *"In the third year of the reign of King Belshazzar a vision appeared to me—to me, Daniel—after the one that appeared to me the first time. I saw in the vision, and it so happened while I was looking, that I was in Shushan, the citadel, which is in the province of Elam; and I saw in the vision that I was by the River Ulai. Then I lifted my eyes and saw, and there, standing beside the river, was a ram which had two horns, and the two horns were high; but one was higher than the other, and the higher one came up last. I saw the ram pushing westward, northward, and southward, so that no animal could withstand him; nor was there any that could deliver from his hand, but he did according to his will and became great. And as I was considering, suddenly a male goat came from the west, across the surface of the whole earth, without touching the ground; and the goat had a notable horn between his eyes. Then he came to the ram that had two horns, which I had seen standing beside the river, and ran at him with furious power."*

The goat with the horn was a man called Alexander the Great, who was an army general and the leader of the Grecian empire in those times. Before that time it was the Medo-persian empire which was symbolised by a ram with two horns: one horn was greater than the other, meaning that one of the two kingdoms that had united to form that empire was stronger than the other.

In Daniel 5:11-12, the Bible describes the nature of the prophetic anointing:

> *"There is a man in your kingdom in whom is the Spirit of the Holy God. And in the days of your father, light and understanding and wisdom, like the wisdom of the gods, were found in him; and King Nebuchadnezzar your father—your father the king—made him chief of*

the magicians, astrologers, Chaldeans, and soothsayers. Inasmuch as an excellent spirit, knowledge, understanding, interpreting dreams, solving riddles, and explaining enigmas were found in this Daniel, whom the king named Belteshazzar, now let Daniel be called, and he will give the interpretation."

Daniel was a prophet with the ability to interpret dreams, which are often full of symbols. He also had the necessary prophetic insight to solve riddles (hard questions) and explain enigmas (mysteries).

Let's read 1 Corinthians 13:2:

"And though I have the gift of prophecy, and understand all mysteries and all knowledge..."

People who have the prophetic office have the ability to understand mysteries, which are hidden secrets. A hidden secret can be found in an image or a symbol, and it takes the anointing of the prophet to decode or crack the puzzle.

1 Corinthians 13 also says that if we have the Gift of Prophecy and understand all mysteries, but we have not got love, then we have nothing. Spiritual gifts are not an end in themselves; walking in love is more important than exercising spiritual gifts. Character development and conformation to the image of Christ are more important.

The third phase of the prophetic word is application. Once we understand the prophecy, we can then do what God is saying.

Chapter 7:

Judging the Prophetic Word and Prophetic Vessel

Not every prophecy comes from God, and not every prophet comes from God. We have to judge the prophetic word and also the prophetic vessel.

7a. Testing the prophetic word

The concept of 'Dualism' is well grounded in the field of theology. It is generally agreed, that there are two opposing forces in God's created universe, even though the forces are not coequal. They have opposite polarities, furthermore one is the creator and the other is a creature. The bible declares that God is good; everything that is good proceeds from God. This assertion is buttressed by James 1:17,where we are told, that every good and perfect gift comes from the Father. John 3:27, also states that a man can receive nothing, except it is given to him from heaven. On the other hand, we are told in John 10:10,that the thief comes, but to steal, and to kill, and to destroy. This statement is a metaphorical one, and is a reference to Satan the originator of all evil. Infact in the mission statement of Jesus in 1 John 3:8b, scripture states that Jesus was manifested to destroy the works of the Devil, whose works were evil.

The concept of dualism by extension of the main dualistic pair already stated is pervasive in the holy writ. There is light as opposed to darkness in John 1:1-3,there is false as opposed to true, truth as opposed to error and many more. The argument as presented so far leads us to a very important premise, the need for testing. If there are true prophecies, then there are also false prophecies. Testing is a very important concept in the scientific world, as well as in everyday life. The electrician will employ a tester to check if there is power in a cable, since one cannot determine this by mere sight. The chemist will use a litmus paper to check a solution for acidity or alkalinity. A nurse will employ test instruments to check if the vital signs of an individual conform to normative patterns. In the same vein when we come over to the realm of the spirit we need testing. The Apostle John said in 1 John 4:1ff, that we should not believe every spirit but we should test the spirits whether they are from God, for false prophets have gone out into the world. In Revelations 2:1ff, he commends the Christians in Ephesus because they had tested those who said they were apostles and were not and had found them liars. The need to test prophecies is well emphasized in the New Testament. In 1 Corinthians 14:29-32, Paul said two or three prophets could speak and others should weigh carefully what is said, this was an inference to the judging of the prophetic word. The word for judge in the Greek New Testament is the word ' krino'. It intimates the making of a decision. If a prophet gives a word, the onus is upon an individual or the church to make a decision whether that word is from God. There has been a lot of abuse in the prophetic movement because of the ignorance among believers in general, they have literally swallowed anything a so called prophet said because it was labeled with the epithet, thus says the Lord. In 1Thessalonians 5:19-22, the Apostle by the Spirit gives the church a series of imperatives. In vs.19, he said we should not quench the Spirit, by this he was indicating that we should make room for charismatic activity within the church. He said we should not despise prophecies, but we should test all things, holding fast to the good and abstaining from the bad. The next logical question then, is how do we test for true prophecies?

The first and most important fact we need to understand is that, any supernatural manifestation or phenomena, may originate from three sources only. It may come from God and His good angelic messengers, or from Satan and his evil emissaries or from the human heart or spirit. A few scriptures will help to make this clear. In Deuteronomy 13:1-5, the bible declares that if a prophet gives a sign and that sign indeed comes to pass but leads one to other gods, that prophet was to be put to death. This shows that the source of that

90

prophecy was not God, even though the sign came to pass. Again in Jeremiah 23:13, the prophet lamented that the prophets of Samaria who were false, because they prophesied by Baal. Baal was a Canaanite deity or an evil spirit. In 16-21, he said the prophets speak a vision of their own hearts and not from the mouth of the Lord. In vs. 21, God sad He had not sent these prophets yet they run, He had not spoken to them yet they prophesied. In vs.28, He said the prophet who has His word must speak it faithfully.

7b.   *Various ways of testing the prophetic word and the prophetic vessel*

Let's look at Jeremiah 23:13-17:

> *"And I have seen folly in the prophets of Samaria: They prophesied by Baal And caused My people Israel to err. Also I have seen a horrible thing in the prophets of Jerusalem: They commit adultery and walk in lies; They also strengthen the hands of evildoers, So that no one turns back from his wickedness. All of them are like Sodom to Me, And her inhabitants like Gomorrah. "Therefore thus says the LORD of hosts concerning the prophets: 'Behold, I will feed them with wormwood, And make them drink the water of gall; For from the prophets of Jerusalem, Profaneness has gone out into all the land.'" Thus says the LORD of hosts: " Do not listen to the words of the prophets who prophesy to you. They make you worthless; They speak a vision of their own heart, Not from the mouth of the LORD. They continually say to those who despise Me, ' The LORD has said, "You shall have peace"'; And to everyone who walks according to the dictates of his own heart, they say, ' No evil shall come upon you"'.*

The source of prophetic inspiration here was not Yahweh, or God – it was demons. Prophecies given by demons will cause people to go astray. Jeremiah 23:16 states that the prophets in question *"... speak a vision of their own heart, not from the mouth of the LORD."* This verse shows that some people prophesy from their own hearts and minds.

Jeremiah 23:25-28 states:

> ""I have heard what the prophets have said who prophesy lies in my name, saying, 'I have dreamed, I have dreamed!' How long will this be in the heart of the prophets who prophesy lies? Indeed they are prophets of the deceit of their own heart, who try to make my people forget my name by their dreams which everyone tells his neighbour, as their fathers forgot My name for Baal. "The prophet who has a dream, let him tell a dream; And he who has My word, let him speak My word faithfully. What is the chaff to the wheat?" says the LORD."

There are so many scripture references about prophets prophesying lies from their own minds and not from God. A person can even give a true prophecy – mentioning your name and all – but it may be from evil spirits and not from God. There are certain demons called familiar spirits, who know people very well. They live within families, spiritually, and as such, they know everything about these families. These spirits can give out information about people, and we need to understand this.

Familiar spirits also know some things that are going to happen in the future, because they planned them, anyway! So if they tell you there is going to be an accident on such-and-such date, guess what? The spirits who planned the accident are the same spirits who showed you the date on which it is going to happen. Bad things do not come from God; everything that is bad comes from the enemy, but everything that is good comes from God (James 1:17).

The fact that a prophecy is true doesn't mean it's from God. In fact, a person can be a true prophesier and a false prophet at the same time, because his life and his character and his ministry show that he is false.

Deuteronomy 13:1-5 states:

> "If there arises among you a prophet or a dreamer of dreams, and he gives you a sign or a wonder, and the sign or the wonder comes to pass, of which he spoke to you, saying, 'Let us go after other gods'—which you have not known—'and let us serve them,' you shall not listen to the

words of that prophet or that dreamer of dreams, for the LORD your God is testing you to know whether you love the LORD your God with all your heart and with all your soul. You shall walk after the LORD your God and fear Him, and keep His commandments and obey His voice; you shall serve Him and hold fast to Him. But that prophet or that dreamer of dreams shall be put to death, because he has spoken in order to turn you away from the LORD your God, who brought you out of the land of Egypt and redeemed you from the house of bondage, to entice you from the way in which the LORD your God commanded you to walk. So you shall put away the evil from your midst."

What this passage is saying is that if a prophet prophesies a dream, vision, sign or wonder, and it comes to pass, that does not necessarily mean it is from God. If after that, the prophet says, *"Let us go after other gods'—which you have not known…"*, it means that both the prophet and his prophecy are leading you away from God. In the Old Testament, such prophets would be put to death.

When you go to any prophetic meeting, check out the prophecies. I am about to show you how to check them out. The tests I list here may not be exhaustive, but they are very helpful in judging the prophetic word.

i.   *Does the prophecy exalt Christ, the Godhead, or man?*

This is the first question you need to ask when a prophecy is spoken. Any prophecy that exalts man is <u>not</u> from the Holy Spirit. In 1 Corinthians 12:1-3, Paul writes:

"Now concerning spiritual gifts, brethren, I do not want you to be ignorant: You know that you were Gentiles, carried away to these dumb idols, however you were led. Therefore I make known to you that no one speaking by the Spirit of God calls Jesus accursed, and no one can say that Jesus is Lord except by the Holy Spirit."

Every true prophecy will exalt Jesus. Let us look at Revelation 19:10:

93

"And I fell at his feet to worship him. But he said to me, "See that you do not do that! I am your fellow servant, and of your brethren who have the testimony of Jesus. Worship God! For the testimony of Jesus is the spirit of prophecy."

We are told in this verse *"... the testimony of Jesus is the spirit of prophecy."* This means that all the Old Testament prophets were talking about one person – Jesus. They were exalting God who came through His son, Christ Jesus, who is the subject of the whole Bible. Jesus was even present in the Old Testament as the pre-incarnate Christ. In Luke 24:44-45, when Jesus walked with some disciples on the road from Jerusalem to Emmaus he made this statement:

"Then He said to them, "These are the words which I spoke to you while I was still with you, that all things must be fulfilled which were written in the Law of Moses and the Prophets and the Psalms concerning Me." And He opened their understanding, that they might comprehend the Scriptures."

The Old Testament was originally written in Hebrew, in three sections: the Law, the Prophets and the Writings. The Law consisted of the Pentateuch, or the five books of Moses. The Prophets consisted of the Major Prophets and the Minor Prophets. The Writings had to do with historical narratives like Judges, Ruth, Psalms, wisdom literature, and so on. Jesus said in Luke 24:44-45, that all these things were about Him. So the Old Testament was speaking about one main character, Jesus.

So you see, every prophecy must exalt or glorify Jesus. He is the centre of every activity in the Church: He is the head of the Church (Colossians 1:15-18). He is the one we worship and serve. He is our Lord and our God. He is God that came to us in the form of man.

Let me repeat this: any prophecy that exalts man cannot be from God. I remember once when I started my church, a man wanted to make my head swell, and he gave a prophecy which said, "Thus saith the Lord, O man of God, prophet Commey, you are the greatest man of God in the whole world..." I made him stop, telling him that this prophecy was not from God, because he was trying to exalt a man, not Christ. As John the Baptist said, *"He must increase, but I must decrease"* (John 3:30).

I told the man that his prophecy was a soulish prophecy, coming from his own mind and heart. In John 3:27 the Bible states: *"A man can receive nothing unless it has been given to him from heaven"*. The Bible also says in 1 Corinthians 4:7 *"And what do you have that you did not receive? Now if you did indeed receive it, why do you boast as if you had not received it?"* In James 1:17 we are told, *"Every good gift and every perfect gift is from above, and comes down from the Father of lights, with whom there is no variation or shadow of turning"*. Personally, I know that by grace, everything I have and everything I am came from God.

In John 16:13, Jesus said:

> *"However, when He, the Spirit of truth, has come, He will guide you into all truth; for He will not speak on His own authority, but whatever He hears He will speak; and He will tell you things to come."*

Even the Holy Spirit depends on Christ to bring messages to us, because the Church belongs to Christ: He is her head. Although the Holy Spirit is also God, and knows everything, He waits for Christ to speak, before He tells us.

ii. *What are the fruits of the prophetic word?*

Anytime we hear about fruits, we must think about seed. As the Bible states in Luke 8:11, *"The seed is the word of God"*. When a prophetic word is sown, it bears fruit, which can be seen, once it has been cultivated. Remember the fruits of the Spirit (Galatians 5:22-23): the Bible says that they are love, joy, peace, longsuffering, kindness, goodness, faithfulness, gentleness and self-control. The works of the flesh, on the other hand, speak of things like division, hatred, murder and so on.

If a word that you have heard is from God, it will edify, exhort,

95

comfort and strengthen you. Does the prophecy make you stronger than when you received it? If it makes you weaker; if it tears you down, then it cannot come from God. Take note, brethren: if any prophecy you receive causes you to backslide, and moves you away from God, then it cannot have come from God.

Likewise, if the word brings you fear; if for instance, it makes you afraid that you will die, then it is not from God. The same goes for a prophecy that intimidates you, says you cannot make it, tells you that you are finished and that there is no more hope. A prophecy that doesn't promote love but divides the Church is not from God. It either came from Satan or from the flesh.

Let me give you an example from the Old Testament, from Deuteronomy 13:1-5:

> *"If there arises among you a prophet or a dreamer of dreams, and he gives you a sign or a wonder, and the sign or the wonder comes to pass, of which he spoke to you, saying, 'Let us go after other gods'—which you have not known—'and let us serve them,' you shall not listen to the words of that prophet or that dreamer of dreams, for the LORD your God is testing you to know whether you love the LORD your God with all your heart and with all your soul. You shall walk after the LORD your God and fear Him, and keep His commandments and obey His voice; you shall serve Him and hold fast to Him. But that prophet or that dreamer of dreams shall be put to death, because he has spoken in order to turn you away from the LORD your God, who brought you out of the land of Egypt and redeemed you from the house of bondage, to entice you from the way in which the LORD your God commanded you to walk. So you shall put away the evil from your midst".*

What this passage is saying is that if a so-called prophet gave a prophecy, and it was detailed and sharp, true and came to pass in the future; but if the prophecy eventually caused people to go astray from God, then that prophet is false, and in the Old Testament, he would have been put to death.

iii. *What are the fruits of the prophetic vessel?*

You can always tell the quality of a fruit by the nature of the seed or the tree that it came from. Therefore, if a prophetic vessel is a bad vessel, you can expect its fruits also to be bad.

Listen, brethren, you should not receive any man and listen to anything he says and go ahead and do it: you need to test it. In fact, even in Acts 17:10, Paul said that when he had taught in Berea, the Berean Christians were very noble and fair-minded, but after even Paul, the great apostle had taught, they went home and checked it out!

In Revelation 2:1-2, John, on the Isle of Patmos, writes what Jesus said:

> *"To the angel of the church of Ephesus write,*
>
> *These things says He who holds the seven stars in His right hand, who walks in the midst of the seven golden lampstands: "I know your works, your labor, your patience, and that you cannot bear those who are evil. And you have tested those who say they are apostles and are not, and have found them liars.""*

Jesus is saying that false apostles are evil. The church of Ephesus tested those who <u>say</u> they are apostles. We can only be tested in God, through His Word. Church leaders can also test an individual to see whether His fruits conform to the Bible, which is the sole authority on earth, for testing spiritual activity.

In Revelation 2:18-23, Jesus says:

> *"And to the angel of the church in Thyatira write,*
>
> *These things says the Son of God, who has eyes like a flame of fire, and His feet like fine brass: "I know your works, love, service, faith, and your patience; and as for your works, the last are more than the first. Nevertheless I have a few things against you, because you allow that woman Jezebel, who calls herself a prophetess, to teach and seduce. My*

servants to commit sexual immorality and eat things sacrificed to idols. And I gave her time to repent of her sexual immorality, and she did not repent. Indeed I will cast her into a sickbed, and those who commit adultery with her into great tribulation, unless they repent of their deeds. I will kill her children with death, and all the churches shall know that I am He who searches the minds and hearts. And I will give to each one of you according to your works.""

Within the above passage, we read the statement, "... *that woman Jezebel, who calls herself a prophetess*" (verse 20). <u>God</u> didn't call Jezebel a prophetess: she didn't qualify to be a prophetess in the eyes of God or in the biblical record.

The latter part of this passage says, "*And I will give to each one of you according to your works*" (verse 23). You see, fellow prophets, we have to be very careful. We have to study the Bible and pray everyday that God will keep us on the righteous path, that we shall be exemplary role models.

Jezebel, we are told, was teaching false doctrines. This is one mark of false prophets – their main doctrine has no biblical foundations. I am not saying that genuine prophets who are not very sound in the Word of God will always teach what is right. Neither will ministers always agree on everything – there are always minor or non-essential areas in which ministers differ (for example, having different perspectives about the events and how they unfold in the book of Revelation), but true prophets will agree on major issues, such as things to do with the blood covenant, salvation, the Holy Spirit, and many others.

None of us is one hundred percent perfect in our doctrine or our life, but this woman had a false status according to scripture. She taught and seduced people to commit sexual immorality. Basically, she taught doctrines of demons. Remember in 1 Timothy 4:1 there is a warning by the Holy Spirit, "*...the Spirit expressly says that in latter times some will depart from the faith, giving heed to deceiving spirits and doctrines of demons...*"

Every man of God has two kinds of fruits: the fruits of his ministry, and the fruits of his life. Both of these have to be checked out. Jesus made a statement about this in Matthew 7:15:

> *"Beware of false prophets, who come to you in sheep's clothing, but inwardly they are ravenous wolves."*

The first thing Jesus says here is, *"Beware of false prophets, who come to you in sheep's clothing…"* (verse15). This means that every false prophet (*pseudoprophetes* in the Greek) will come pretending to be a true prophet. They will come <u>like</u> true prophets, will talk <u>like</u> true prophets, and will quote scriptures <u>like</u> true prophets, but their character will betray them.

We are the sheep of God's pasture; a sheep is a symbol of a Christian, and it refers to meekness and humility. If a false prophet came into our midst, and he was a wolf, all the sheep would scatter, because they would see him as an enemy. But false prophets who are used by demons have demonic wisdom. They do not present themselves like wolves. They dress like sheep, just like other people in the Church. So when they come among the real sheep, it is difficult for us to detect them. If we subject them to the test, then we can find out whether they are really from God or not.

Jesus says that "inwardly" (on the inside: it takes God to show us the inside of a man), false prophets are like wolves. What do wolves do? Wolves chew up and destroy other animals. If a false prophet came to your church, your church would be destroyed, if you are not careful. The false prophet will destroy the sheep.

Matthew 7:16 states, *"You will know them by their fruits. Do men gather grapes from thorn bushes or figs from thistles?"*. You won't know them by their prophecies, because their prophecies might be accurate. They can say to you, "Your name is John", and this will be true, because the familiar spirit who gave them the information knows that your name is John.

When we see a prophet, we must look first at his fruits, before we look at his prophecy. We should look at the fruit of love, the fruits of kindness, compassion, good works, right living, and more. He shouldn't love money – which is one of the signs of false prophets, who sometimes charge people for giving prophecies. Find out about the prophet's track record, and ask about him from other pastors who know him, before you do the things he is telling you to do.

In Matthew 7:18-19, Jesus says:

> "A good tree cannot bear bad fruit, nor can a bad tree bear good fruit. Every tree that does not bear good fruit is cut down and thrown into the fire."

Here Jesus is saying that people stand the risk of going to hell if they continue with this bad fruit – if they continue using the ministry as a means of making money, or if they lead people astray. This is a warning of judgement from Jesus Himself. We all have to be careful: we have to pray that we will be true representatives from God until we depart from this earth to be with the Lord.

Jesus adds in Matthew 7:22:

> "Many will say to Me in that day, 'Lord, Lord, have we not prophesied in Your name, cast out demons in Your name, and done many wonders in Your name?'"

By now you should have realised that the fact that you prophesy doesn't mean that you will go to heaven. You can prophesy and do many mighty works and still end up in hell. It is your fruit and your character that God is looking at. That is why I pray everyday, "Lord, let my character conform to the Bible". I tell all my church members to pray that my character will be sound throughout my life. I want to be a good role model; I want to be God's true representative. You also have to pray like that, for God to keep you.

The Bible says in 2 Peter 1 that we are kept by the power of God through faith. God can keep us from messing up. May the Lord keep you and I until we see Him face-to-face on the last day.

Let us not be like those who Jesus was addressing in Matthew 7:23, *"And then I will declare to them, 'I never knew you; depart from me, you who practice lawlessness!"* When Jesus says, "depart", it means you are going to hell. The prophets Jesus was referring to were found to have been practising lawlessness. They didn't follow the Bible, and they didn't live their lives according to the scriptures. 1 John 3:4 states that sin is lawlessness. We are told that every unrighteousness is sin (1 John 5:17).

iv. *If it is a prediction, does it come to pass?*

It is not everything that is said to happen in the future that is true and will come to pass, but if a prediction comes to pass, it may be a sign that God has spoken. I am not saying that every prediction that comes to pass is from God. As I said earlier, sometimes there are satanic predictions that come to pass, especially where satanic powers themselves have planned an event in the future.

As I have said already, if you don't pray, don't fast, and don't co-operate with God, your prophecy might not come to pass. But there are some prophecies that you are given, where you have done everything that is right, and they still do not come to pass. This may be due to the fact the prophecy or prediction didn't come from God in the first place.
Deuteronomy 18:18-22 states:

> *"I will raise up for them a Prophet like you from among their brethren, and will put My words in His mouth, and He shall speak to them all that I command Him. And it shall be that whoever will not hear My words, which He speaks in My name, I will require it of him. But the prophet who presumes to speak a word in My name, which I have not commanded him to speak, or who speaks in the name of other gods, that prophet shall die.' And if you say in your heart, 'How shall we know the word which the LORD has not spoken?'— when a prophet speaks*

in the name of the LORD, if the thing does not happen or come to pass, that is the thing which the LORD has not spoken; the prophet has spoken it presumptuously; you shall not be afraid of him."

Every prophet must be careful to wait for the Word of God to come to him or her, before giving a word of prophecy. Don't be presumptuous: make sure you don't say something out of your own mind.

I am always careful to say what the Holy Spirit gives me to say, and the prophecies I give come to pass because I heard right, and because I waited to hear from God before speaking. When people call me, saying, "What you said has come to pass", I always give them a point of correction. I tell them, "I didn't say those things, because if I said those things, they couldn't have come to pass, since I am only a mortal man!"

There is only one true God in the person of the Father, and one Lord, in the person of Jesus Christ. All other gods are fake. There is only one-way to heaven: Jesus said, *"I am the way, the truth, and the life. No one comes to the Father except through Me"* (John 14:6). In Acts 4:12 we read, *"Nor is there salvation in any other, for there is no other name under heaven given among men by which we must be saved."*

With some of us, once we see a man of God, we begin to shiver with awe, and we are prepared to do anything he tells us. If he even says, "Go and steal", you steal, thinking it must be from God! How can God tell you to steal money? You must test the prophet.

V. *Does it bear witness with your spirit?*

As I said earlier, any prophecy you receive must bear witness with your spirit. You also have the Holy Spirit, so you have what it takes to check out the prophecy. If you get a prophecy that makes you feel unhappy, troubled, distressed, or fearful, throw it out. Most of the time, it's not from God.

Let's look at Romans 8:14-16:

> *"For as many as are led by the Spirit of God, these are sons of God.*
> *For you did not receive the spirit of bondage again to fear, but you*
> *received the Spirit of adoption by whom we cry out, "Abba, Father."*
> *The Spirit Himself bears witness with our spirit that we are children of*
> *God."*

The Holy Spirit bears witness with our spirits that we are children of
God. In the same way, if someone claims to prophesy to you by the
Holy Spirit, then that same Holy Spirit must witness with your spirit,
and say, "Yes, my child, this is from me". But if it troubles your spirit,
then you know that it is not from God.

God says that you must not fear; any prophecy that makes you fear is
not from God. 2 Timothy 1:7 says:

> *"For God has not given us a spirit of fear, but of power and of love and*
> *of a sound mind."*

Any prophetic word received from a false prophet will put you in
bondage, enslaving you in a spiritual prison.

The Holy Spirit himself will bear witness that we are children of God,
but you must be a very prayerful Christian – so that your spirit is sharp
– to be able to discern when something is wrong, and to be able to
hear when God speaks. If a prophetic word comes to you, the Holy
Spirit will bear witness as to whether it is from God or not.

If your spirit rejects a prophecy, then it means that God is giving you a
warning, and you should not proceed.

vi. *Is the prophecy compatible with the written Word of God?*

Any prophecy that contradicts scripture (the "Logos") is not from
God. Throw it out immediately. I once heard a joke, that somebody

prophesied, "My people, my people, my people, I am with you, do not be afraid – even though I myself am sometimes afraid."

Tell me, how can God be afraid? Such a prophecy cannot be from God. You must judge prophecies by listening to them and checking them out with the Bible, to see whether they contradict or conform to the written Word of God. Even if the prophecy lines up with scripture, that does not mean that it is from God. You have to do some other checks.

Let us look at some examples from scripture, beginning with Isaiah 8:19-20:

> *"And when they say to you, "Seek those who are mediums and wizards, who whisper and mutter," should not a people seek their God? Should they seek the dead on behalf of the living? To the law and to the testimony! If they do not speak according to this word, it is because there is no light in them."*

The Bible is saying here concerning the Israelites, that they should not seek familiar spirits or demonic agents, but they should seek the counsel of God through the Word of God. The Bible says, *"To the Law and to the testimony"* (Isaiah 8:20) (the Law referred to here is the *Torah*, the Hebrew Bible).

God is saying that if someone comes to you claiming to be a prophet, but he cannot preach the word, cannot teach the Bible, and cannot speak according to God's Word, then forget about him. There is no light in him, and therefore he is full of darkness: the wrong character and the wrong fruit are in that person.

Every prophet must study the Bible very well. I am still studying biblical Greek, because I want to know more of what the Bible is saying, so that I can be a good teacher and show the people of God the right thing that God is saying. We have to study to show ourselves approved unto God, workmen who need not be ashamed, rightly dividing the word of truth (2 Timothy 2:15).

In 1 John 5:7, the scripture states:

"For there are three that bear witness in heaven: the Father, the Word, and the Holy Spirit; and these three are one."

This means that whatever the Father is saying, is what the Word is saying (the Word is Jesus Christ – the Living Word), and it is also what the Holy Spirit is saying. The three are in harmony.

The Holy Spirit wrote the Bible through human vessels. We are told in 2 Timothy 3:16-17 that *"...all Scripture is given by inspiration of God, and is profitable for doctrine, for reproof, for correction, for instruction in righteousness, that the man of God may be complete, thoroughly equipped for every good work"*. So, if the Holy Spirit is behind the Bible, and He actually moved or inspired the biblical authors to write the Bible, it means that nothing inspired by the Holy Spirit can contradict the scriptures.

A prophecy that comes by the Holy Spirit cannot contradict the Word of God.

vii. *Is there a corporate witness?*

Most of the time, after you have been given a prophecy, you must not try to run with it, until you have got another witness – for example, someone else prophesying the same thing, or confirming the prophecy. If you receive a prophecy and no one has said the same thing to you before, or if God has not given you the same message already, you should probably put it on the shelf. If you even had prior knowledge of the subject, and another prophet had also said it, it means you have two witnesses, and you can go ahead and do that which the prophet said.

If you had no prior knowledge of the message, and this is the first time you are hearing about it, you have to pray and ask God for another confirmation. You especially need help from Church leaders – sound men of God who also have the Holy Spirit. You must submit your prophecy to them, so that they will judge it and see whether it is truly from God. This is the corporate witness.

Let us look at 2 Corinthians 13:1:

> *"This will be the third time I am coming to you. "By the mouth of two or three witnesses every word shall be established."*

In mathematics, you cannot plot a straight or linear graph with only one coordinate, one *xy*. You need two points to be able to draw a line. So we see that a line is fixed by at least two points (*x1y1* passing through *x2y2*). The same goes for prophecy. You need two or three witnesses to confirm a prophecy.

viii. *Does the prophecy edify and build up the hearer, or does it tear the person down?*

Is the prophecy discouraging? There are some prophecies that reveal what Satan is doing. If such a prophecy is from God, the prophet will let you know that although the enemy may be planning an accident or something bad, God has revealed to redeem – He will deliver you from it. So you do not need to be afraid. But any prophecy that comes to scare you and gives you no hope will not be from God.

Chapter 8:

The Prophetic Office

8a.   Definition of the Prophetic Office

Today, all over the world there are many who call themselves prophets. In this section, we will answer the question, "Who is a prophet?" in great detail, and from the Biblical perspective.

Jesus asked the Pharisees a question in Matthew 21:25-27. He said:

> *"The baptism of John—where was it from? From heaven or from men?" And they reasoned among themselves, saying, "If we say, 'From heaven,' He will say to us, 'Why then did you not believe him?' But if we say, 'From men,' we fear the multitude, for all count John as a prophet." So they answered Jesus and said, "We do not know." And He said to them, "Neither will I tell you by what authority I do these things."*

Jesus' question elicits some very important things. He asked if John's prophetic ministry was from heaven or from earth. In other words, was John made a prophet by himself or by men? Or, was it God who declared him a prophet?

When anyone says that he or she is a prophet, we need to check from heaven, to see if heaven knows him or her. In other words, does this person qualify to be called a prophet? Remember, there are qualifications for a prophet in the Bible. In fact, there are even qualifications for leadership in the Bible.

I am not saying that anyone can fulfil every requirement one hundred percent, but at least, those in leadership, or those who are recognised as having the ministry gifts, should have <u>most</u> of these attributes. All the major attributes will be present in a mature man or woman of God. Remember, the ministry gifts (including the prophet) are only for people who are mature in God.

Ephesians 4:11 says:

> *"And He Himself gave some to be apostles, some prophets, some evangelists, and some pastors and teachers."*

This is what we call the Universal Church Leadership. These are leaders, not novices or inexperienced people. They are not for the young in the faith; they are for mature people in the faith, people who have been walking with Jesus for a long time; people who have been taught, schooled and educated in the scriptures to such an extent that they can also teach others. These are people who are qualified to become prophets.

So you see, if anyone calls himself a prophet, and he does not measure up to these criteria, the Bible rejects him as a prophet. It may be, though, that the person is *called* to become a prophet, but he is not yet a prophet. He may already manifest prophetic gifts, but that alone will not make him a prophet. In fact, he can prophesy accurately and even raise the dead - it doesn't matter. This is just spiritual gifts in operation, and any Christian can manifest spiritual gifts. Spiritual gifts do not make a person mature.

To give an example, in 1 Corinthians 1:7, Paul wrote to the Corinthians and said, *"...so that you come short in no gift"*. In other words, the Corinthian church had all the spiritual gifts as far as biblical record is concerned. There was so much prophetic activity that we are told in 1 Corinthians 14:29, *"Let two or three prophets speak, and let the others judge"*. There were a lot of people prophesying in their midst.

Though the people in the Corinthian church were very charismatic and operated spiritual gifts, Paul said something to them that is very important in helping us to understand this discussion. In 1 Corinthians

108

3:1-2, Paul says:

> *"And I, brethren, could not speak to you as to spiritual people but as to carnal, as to babes in Christ. I fed you with milk and not with solid food; for until now you were not able to receive it, and even now you are still not able…"*

Milk is the symbol for elementary doctrines, for people who are not mature in Christ, and for people who are not educated in the Word of God. They only feed on milk. Solid food, on the other hand, is symbolic for advanced doctrine. This is for people who are mature. Paul was saying to the Corinthians that even though they prophesied in detail and everything they said comes to pass, they were still babies: they could not be leaders. They themselves needed to be taught and led, because they were not mature.

In the Old Testament, there are various phrases used for a prophet. One of them is "a man of God". We read phrases like, "a man of God went from Judah to Bethel" (1 Kings 13:1). The Hebrew phrase for "a man of God" is *ish Elohim*, meaning "a man who represents God" or "a man who represents the Word of God". If a man does not know God's Word, how then can he represent God ? How, therefore, can he be a prophet? He is not qualified to be a prophet.

Remember, maturity in Christ comes through knowledge and understanding, not by gifts. I have heard people say, "This man is a great man of God". I ask why, and they say, "Look at the gifts, how powerful he is". The extent of a man's power is not the extent of his maturity. Understanding and growth in Christ come only through the Word of God.

Remember, 1 Peter 2:2 says, *"As newborn babes, desire the pure milk of the word, that you may grow thereby…"* The only way a man can grow to become a leader is through serious studying of the scriptures. When I became born-again at the age of twenty, I read the Bible from cover to cover several times: I was so hungry for the Word of God. The Bible says that Jesus said in the beatitudes in Matthew 5:6, *"Blessed are those who hunger and thirst for righteousness, for they shall be filled".* I prayed and studied, and in no time, I started teaching in church.

Let me give you the general qualifications for leadership in the Church. Remember, the prophet is a leader, just as the apostle, teacher, pastor and evangelist. 1 Timothy 3:1-7 lists the necessary qualifications:

> *"This is a faithful saying: If a man desires the position of a bishop, he desires a good work. A bishop then must be blameless, the husband of one wife, temperate, sober-minded, of good behaviour, hospitable, able to teach; not given to wine, not violent, not greedy for money, but gentle, not quarrelsome, not covetous; one who rules his own house well, having his children in submission with all reverence (for if a man does not know how to rule his own house, how will he take care of the church of God?); not a novice, lest being puffed up with pride he fall into the same condemnation as the devil. Moreover he must have a good testimony among those who are outside, lest he fall into reproach and the snare of the devil."*

The word "Bishop" here means "pastor" or "overseer". The Greek word is *episkopos*, meaning "one who oversees a congregation or a flock". We can also render the translation as "pastor". We are told that a Bishop must be a man against whom no bad accusation can be proved. Men of God many times have people say bad things about them; sometimes bad things are published in the media about them, but most of the accusations are not true. The smear campaign against ministers is the work of satanic spirits.
In 2 Corinthians 6, Paul talks about the fact that if you are going to minister, be sure to expect good and evil reports about you. But when we get evil reports spread about us, those accusations must not be proven to be true.

God says that a bishop should be the husband of one wife. How therefore, can somebody with five wives claim to be a prophet? In the Old Testament, God permitted the patriarchs to have several wives, but that was not the perfect will of God. He only 'permitted' them. Remember they asked for a king: God permitted them to have a king, but it wasn't the perfect will of God for Israel to have a king at the time that they made the request.

In the Old Testament, people did not have the Holy Spirit in them, and therefore, they did not have the power to live holy lives. Even though God used them mightily because He had anointed them, they faltered many times. We know about David, for instance, about how he messed up.

We of the New Testament are also not infallible. Remember, 1 John 2 says that if we sin, we have an advocate with the Father, Jesus Christ the righteous, by whose blood our sins will be wiped away. This means that we still sin and make mistakes, even under the New Testament.

God allowed the Old Testament men to marry many wives because they could not keep the Law. We mustn't say that because David and Solomon had many wives, we must also do the same. There is a higher standard in the New Testament – we are under grace. God has given us the power to live righteously. It would be contrary to the scriptures if a bishop had more than one wife.

A bishop must also be temperate, that is, self-controlled. A self-controlled man of God knows when to read his Bible and when to pray; he is mature and has got himself together. He is sober-minded, of good behaviour, hospitable and able to teach. As said earlier, if a man is not able to teach, he cannot claim to be a prophet. Prophets represent the Word of God, and as such, they have to be able to teach and/or preach.

Bishops should not be drunkards, violent, or greedy for money. A Christian leader must not love money at all. A bishop should also be gentle, not quarrelsome and not covetous. He should rule his house well, having his children in submission with all reverence. If a man does not know how to rule his own house, how can he take care of the Church of God?

The Bible also says in 1 Timothy 3:6, that a bishop should not be a novice. The word "novice" is from the word "neophyte", which means newly planted, inexperienced and immature. Many young people who say that they are prophets are eventually tempted with pride because they will not submit to leadership and authority. They leave to start their own ministries, and because of their spiritual gifts, people follow them and give them money, which results in these young people being filled with pride. Many of them fall in the same way that the devil fell.

The bishop should also have a good testimony among those who are outside the Church, lest he fall into reproach and the snare of the devil.

8b. The status of the prophet in the Old Testament

As I said earlier, the prophetic movement started right from the beginning of creation. Luke 1:67-70 talks about the fact that God speaks through His holy prophets who have been since the world began. Prophetic ministry is therefore the oldest ministry, but the prophet of the Old Testament is not the same as the prophet of the New Testament. There are similarities and dissimilarities. One needs to know those differences, since we sometimes find people under the New Testament covenant operating like Old Testament prophets. That is because we have not studied to find out the nature of the ministry of the prophets in the two testaments.

In the Old Testament, there were only three offices: the priest, the prophet and the king. The Holy Spirit anointed these people. The rest of the people had no Holy Spirit presence in them, but God would occasionally anoint somebody for a particular work. For instance, we are told about Bezalel, the son of Uri. He was a designer, and he helped Moses build the tabernacle (Exodus 35:30-35). The Holy Spirit came upon him for that specific project, and afterwards, the Holy Spirit left. The people did not have any tangible presence of the Holy Spirit in them that was residential or indwelling.

We who are in the New Testament have the privilege of having Christ dwell in our hearts through faith, and we have the Holy Spirit indwelling us. So the office of the prophet in the Old Testament will differ from that in the New Testament.

Let me show you the characteristics of the prophetic office of the Old Testament. Remember, we had many prophets who prophesied in the Old Testament, some of whom are not named, and some of whom were major prophets like Elijah and Elisha. Elijah and Elisha were great prophets who did signs and wonders and miracles, but they did not write books in the Bible. There were also the writing prophets, those who wrote books containing different kinds of prophecies. We are even told in Genesis 20:7, that Abraham was a prophet.

We therefore had different kinds of prophets with different profiles and different assignments and callings. The primary thing about the Old Testament prophets is that the people went to them for guidance, to enquire of them. In fact, kings would not go to war until they had consulted the prophets.
In 1 Kings 22, we are told that King Jehoshaphat went to consult a prophet called Micaiah, and in 2 Kings 3:4-12, we are told that the King of Israel, the King of Judah and the King of Edom teamed up together and went to Elisha the prophet to enquire of God about a battle that they were going to fight.

In the Old Testament, people consulted prophets to make critical decisions in life, but in the New Testament, we do not do that any longer. Remember, the people in the Old Testament did not have the Holy Spirit in them for guidance, per se. But now, we have the Holy Spirit in us for guidance. In Romans 8:14 the Bible says:

"For as many as are led by the Spirit of God, these are sons of God."

Now we have the capacity to know the will of God for our lives, through what we call the *inner witness*, listening to the Holy Sprit who indwells us. That does not mean that we no longer need prophets - prophets still have their place.

Another thing is that in the Old Testament, when the prophets prophesied, their prophetic words were not tested per se. They were mature men with experience, and we are told in Deuteronomy 13:1-5 that prophets who gave false prophecies were sometimes stoned to death. So prophesying was not child's play – in those days it was not at all for young, immature people.

Even though the Old Testament prophet was not tested per se, the Bible says in Deuteronomy 18:20, that if a prophet gave a prediction that did not come to pass, it meant that he had not spoken from the Lord. So when Old Testament prophets said, "Thus saith the Lord", they really meant it! This is different from now, in the New Testament era, where the Bible urges us to judge every prophetic word since we also have the Holy Spirit inside us, and we can witness whether something being said is of God or not.

Here are some more points about Old Testament prophets:

1. They were the preachers of the day. Every prophet had a preaching anointing, and they all preached. Some were sent to the Northern Kingdom and some were sent to the Southern Kingdom. Others were sent to both.

2. They were reformers. Many times during the history of the Israelites, the people were in sin. They were worshipping idols and had left the true God Yahweh. In these times the prophets were needed to preach messages, which were usually about sin, repentance and judgement. One example can be seen in 1 Kings 18:21 when Elijah called a contest between himself and the prophets of Baal on Mount Carmel, because the people of God had gone astray to serve idols. Elijah said:

"How long will you falter between two opinions? If the LORD is God, follow Him; but if Baal, follow him."

Elijah did dramatic signs and wonders, calling fire from heaven. And the people said, *"The LORD, He is God!"* (verse 39), and they repented.

3. Old Testament prophets were what we call "covenant enforcement mediators". They never preached anything by themselves; they only preached what God had already said in the past. Remember, God had given them the Ten Commandments, and God gave in Deuteronomy 28 and some of the Old Testament passages, blessings for obedience and curses for disobedience. The Old Testament prophets made sure that God's law was adhered to.

4. They predicted the coming of the Messiah. Some of the content of the Old Testament books is highly messianic. Many of the prophets in the Old Testament prophesied about the coming of Christ. Even in Psalm 22, David gives a graphic description about how the Messiah would be crucified on the cross. Some of the Old Testament prophets saw the Messiah as a king, and some of them saw him as a servant. They saw different pictures of the Messiah before he burst forth on the scene.

5. They often spoke of a coming day of judgement, called The Day of the Lord. The book of Zephaniah and others talk about The Day of the Lord.

6. They had the power of the Holy Spirit upon them: they had supernatural endowment. The revelation and power gifts were regularly manifested in their ministries.

7. The kings and the people of Israel regularly enquired of the prophets before making critical decisions.

8c. The status of the prophet in the New Testament

In the New Testament, the prophetic office differs slightly from the Old Testament, although all prophets use the same tools, the same

Gifts of the Spirit. The only gifts, which were not in operation in the Old Testament, were the Gift of Tongues and the Gift of Interpretation of Tongues.

All the other gifts were present: the Word of Wisdom, Word of Knowledge, Discerning of Spirits, Gift of Faith, Gift of Healing, Gift of Miracles and Gift of Prophecy.

Another difference from the Old Testament is that under the New Testament, one doesn't have to primarily seek guidance from prophets anymore. Now, born-again Christians seek guidance from God directly, by praying and by listening to the Holy Spirit, who is inside us. If God chooses to lead us to a prophet, so be it. Remember, the Bible says, *"As many as are led by the Spirit, these are the sons of God"* (Romans 8:14).

While in the Old Testament, the people went to prophets for guidance, in the New Testament; the prophet goes to the people - to the churches. Since prophecy is to edify the Church, today's prophets are travelling ministers.

For example, Acts 11:27-30 states:

> *"And in these days prophets came from Jerusalem to Antioch. Then one of them, named Agabus, stood up and showed by the Spirit that there was going to be a great famine throughout all the world, which also happened in the days of Claudius Caesar. Then the disciples, each according to his ability, determined to send relief to the brethren dwelling in Judea. This they also did, and sent it to the elders by the hands of Barnabas and Saul."*

This passage shows prophets travelling from Jerusalem to Antioch. If you read Acts 21:7-11, you will see that Agabus had once travelled to Caesarea, to the house of Philip the evangelist, who had four daughters who prophesied.

So in the New Testament, prophets go to the churches to strengthen them, give counsel, direction and correction, and they reveal the plans of God. But we don't need to go to prophets and ask, "I want to travel to London. Must I go or not?" That is not what prophets are called to do at this time.

The New Testament prophet is primarily a teacher and/or preacher of the Word. That is why, if you want to know who are the prophets in this New Testament era, the first thing you must look at is the fruit of their ministry: how they teach, how they preach, whether they are sound in doctrine, and whether they are established and rooted in the Word. If not, they are not qualified to be prophets.

Remember, the Bible says in 2 Timothy 2:15, *"Be diligent to present yourself approved to God, a worker who does not need to be ashamed, rightly dividing the word of truth."* In 2 Timothy 3:16-17, Paul says:

> *"All Scripture is given by inspiration of God, and is profitable for doctrine, for reproof, for correction, for instruction in righteousness, that the man of God may be complete, thoroughly equipped for every good work."*

Once again, I must stress, you cannot be a man of God if you don't know God's Word. What are you going to tell the people? Prophetic ministry is not just prophesying: prophesying is a minor role. The main part is raising people – equipping saints, as the Bible says in Ephesians 4:11-12, as we read earlier on:

> *"And He Himself gave some to be apostles, some prophets, some evangelists, and some pastors and teachers."*

The Bible never said that God gave some evangelists, etc. for the prophesying to the saints. It never said that! It said *"...for the equipping of the saints"* (verse 12). Of course, prophecy is an integral part of the equipping, but it is not the main part. The primary duty or purpose of a prophet is that he must be able to teach sound doctrine, and to teach the Word. In fact, the teaching and preaching ministry of a prophet is normally very unusual; it carries greater insight than normal, because it is a high-level office. It is not for the immature or the novice.

The New Testament prophet also activates gifts and ministries. This means that prophets are very passionate about God's plan for the Church and for the lives of individuals. Often, when they come to your church, they can spot you and know what call is on your life. Many times when I see people I can tell who is an evangelist, who is a prophet, who will be a prophet, who will be a businessman, and so on. I know it by just looking at them under the anointing.

We arrange the soldiers of the cross; we arrange the body of Christ for war. We know what position you must stand in, and we know what God has determined concerning your life. We prophets have that ability and grace. Sometimes, if one doesn't know his or her gift, if a prophet lays hands on you and prays for you, the gift inside you will begin to manifest. It will be stirred up under the prophetic anointing. Other times, one may have gone astray, into the wrong ministry, and a prophet can tell him or her. New Testament prophets have that ability, and it is part of their calling.

Next, the New Testament prophets engage in forth telling and fore telling, just as their Old Testament counterparts. As we have already seen, forth telling has to do with preaching. One prominent Greek scholar said - while defining the prophetic office - that prophets speak from the light, or impulse, of a sudden revelation. Sometimes prophets can stop in the middle of their preaching and give a message to somebody. Fore telling, or predicting the future also comes through the Gift of the Word of Wisdom.

8d.   The prophetic anointing

The New Testament Church is prophetic, as seen in Joel 2:28. This is due to the indwelling Spirit of God. We are all able to engage in prophetic listening and proclamation in different degrees, but not all are called to be prophets.

In 1 Corinthians 12:18, the Bible says that God has placed the members in the body just as he pleases. And in 1 Corinthians 12:28, the Bible says God has set in the Church first, apostles, secondly prophets. So God has not set everybody as a prophet. In fact, we are asked in 1 Corinthians 12:29, *"Are all prophets?"* And the answer is "No".

A prophet operates under the prophetic anointing, which is the supernatural power, inspiration and ability that comes upon a prophet to prophesy. Later on I will go more into detail about the Gift of Prophecy the prophet utilises, so that you can understand how prophets receive their messages, and how they are able to know what will happen in the future.

Ordinarily, a prophet, when walking on the street, has not got the prophetic anointing upon him. Although the prophetic anointing can come upon a prophet at any time, as the Lord wills, the prophetic anointing normally comes upon him when he starts to minister.

In some meetings where the prophet goes, the environment is such that the prophet does not sense the presence of God. In those cases, there are some things the prophet can do to create a prophetic atmosphere.

Firstly, the prophetic anointing can be provoked through music. An example of this can be found in 2 Kings 3:11-15.

"But Jehoshaphat said, "Is there no prophet of the LORD here, that we may inquire of the LORD by him?"

So one of the servants of the king of Israel answered and said, "Elisha the son of Shaphat is here, who poured water on the hands of Elijah." And Jehoshaphat said, "The word of the LORD is with him." So the king of Israel and Jehoshaphat and the king of Edom went down to him. Then Elisha said to the king of Israel, "What have I to do with you? Go to the prophets of your father and the prophets of your mother." But the king of Israel said to him, "No, for the LORD has called these three kings together to deliver them into the hand of Moab." And Elisha said, "As the LORD of hosts lives, before whom I stand, surely were it not that I regard the presence of Jehoshaphat king of Judah, I would not look at you, nor see you. But now bring me a musician." Then it happened, when the musician played, that the hand of the LORD came upon him."

As Elisha did in 2 Kings 3, every prophet must wait to sense the prophetic anointing, before going on to minister: otherwise he might prophesy out of his mind, and not out of the Holy Ghost. The prophetic anointing is therefore an indication that a prophet is ready to deliver the accurate Word of God.

When there is good and inspiring music, the prophetic anointing increases, and one can easily prophesy powerfully and for a long time. Music is also used as a medium to provoke the healing anointing. In the above passage, Elisha saw that he wasn't getting the anointing that he needed: the inspiration level was too low to go into prophecy. So he asked for a musician.

The second way, in which the prophetic anointing can be provoked, is through worship. In Acts 13:1-3, we read:

"Now in the church that was at Antioch there were certain prophets and teachers: Barnabas, Simeon who was called Niger, Lucius of Cyrene, Manaen who had been brought up with Herod the tetrarch, and Saul. As they ministered to the Lord and fasted, the Holy Spirit said, "Now separate to Me Barnabas and Saul for the work to which I have called them." Then, having fasted and prayed, and laid hands on them, they sent them away."

You can see here that there were prophets and teachers in the church at Antioch. They fasted, prayed and ministered to the Lord. The word "ministered" here pertains to worship. They were worshipping God, and that provoked the prophetic anointing. I believe that the Spirit energised one of the prophets present, and he began to prophesy about the calling of Paul and Barnabas. That ushered them into a great missionary call.

Thirdly, the prophetic anointing can be provoked through prayer and fasting. I have given you some earlier examples of this, but let's look now at 2 Kings 6:15-17. This passage speaks of how Elisha was giving prophecies to the King of Israel, about the war plans of the Syrians. Let's read from verses 8 to 15:

> *"Now the king of Syria was making war against Israel; and he consulted with his servants, saying, "My camp will be in such and such a place." And the man of God sent to the king of Israel, saying, "Beware that you do not pass this place, for the Syrians are coming down there." Then the king of Israel sent someone to the place of which the man of God had told him. Thus he warned him, and he was watchful there, not just once or twice. Therefore the heart of the king of Syria was greatly troubled by this thing; and he called his servants and said to them, "Will you not show me which of us is for the king of Israel?" And one of his servants said, "None, my lord, O king; but Elisha, the prophet who is in Israel, tells the king of Israel the words that you speak in your bedroom." So he said, "Go and see where he is, that I may send and get him." And it was told him, saying, "Surely he is in Dothan." Therefore he sent horses and chariots and a great army there, and they came by night and surrounded the city. And when the servant of the man of God arose early and went out, there was an army, surrounding the city with horses and chariots. And his servant said to him, "Alas, my master! What shall we do?"*

The servant of the prophet Elisha was afraid, because an army battalion had surrounded their houses to kill Elisha. The servant was so fearful, that he said, "Alas my master, what shall we do?" Elisha told his servant in verse 16:

> *"Do not fear, for those who are with us are more than those who are with them."*

Verse 17 says:
> *"And Elisha prayed, and said, "LORD, I pray, open his eyes that he*

may see." Then the LORD opened the eyes of the young man, and he saw. And behold, the mountain was full of horses and chariots of fire all around Elisha."

It was this prayer that provoked a prophetic anointing on Elisha's servant, and enabled him to enter the spiritual realm to see for himself angels all around that had come to protect and defend them.

Chapter 9:

The New Testament Prophet

The prophet is a ministry gift, so if we want to study the New Testament Prophet, we must study this subject in the broader context of the purpose of church leaders. As leaders, the apostle, prophet, evangelist, pastor and teacher have many things in common.

9a.   The ministry gifts in the New Testament

We are told in Ephesians 4:8-12 that when Christ ascended on high, he gave gifts to men. He gave some apostles, some prophets, some evangelists, some pastors and teachers, for the perfecting and maturing of the saints for the work of the ministry and the edifying of the body of Christ.

As mentioned above, in charismatic circles we have various terms for these people. We call them "Church Leadership", "Governmental Offices", "Headship Ministries", or "the Ascension Gifts of Christ". The word "governmental" means that they have the ability, power and maturity to rule or govern in the Church.

Young people cannot govern (though they may have outstanding spiritual gifts), as they do not yet have the wisdom, ability, maturity and grace. They have not yet been properly trained or equipped.

I cannot take a boy of sixteen years and make him the head of a whole organisation. He would not have the wisdom and maturity. Likewise, I cannot take an immature boy of twenty years, and make him the head of a church! Such a young boy would have to be mentored and overseen so that he will not go astray. If he is left to his own devices and he goes to plant a church, he would cause trouble and lead people astray.

The ministry gifts are also called "the Ascension Gifts of Christ", since it was when Christ ascended that He gave part of Himself as an apostle, part as a prophet, part as an evangelist, part as a pastor, and part as a teacher.

Let me give brief definitions of each of the ministry gifts, starting with the apostle. The word "apostle" is from the Greek word *apostolos*, which means "one who is sent with a commission". The Greek word *pempo also* means "to send", but *apostello* means "to send with a commission". From this, we have the derived noun, *apostolos*, which means "one who is sent with a commission".

An apostle is an ambassador. In the secular world, we can have an ambassador of Ghana to America. When he goes to America, he will present his credentials to the receiving authority, giving details of his mission. During his tenure in America, he cannot do what he likes; he has to do only what the Ghanaian government has instructed him to do. Likewise, Christ sends apostles and gives them a commission – what to do, where to go, what to say.

Apostles have the ability to initiate ministries. They can plant churches easily, because of the apostolic anointing upon them. They birth new works. No wonder Paul said in 1 Corinthians 3:6, *"I planted, Apollos watered, but God gave the increase".* An apostle has the ability to plant, but someone else does the watering. As such, apostles are foundation layers. Paul said in 1 Corinthians 3:10-13:

> *"According to the grace of God which was given to me, as a wise master builder I have laid the foundation, and another builds on it. But let each one take heed how he builds on it. For no other foundation can anyone lay than that which is laid, which is Jesus Christ. Now if anyone builds on this foundation with gold, silver, precious stones, wood, hay, straw, each one's work will become clear; for the Day will declare it, because it*

will be revealed by fire; and the fire will test each one's work, of what sort it is."

Apostles also have the ability to train and equip leaders. In the Old Testament, there were no apostles, but rather types of apostles: people who were like apostles. Solomon was an apostolic type because he built the Temple.

Jesus was the first apostle. In Hebrews 3:1, we are told that He is the apostle and a high priest of our confession. In John 20:21, Jesus said, *"Peace to you! As the Father has sent Me, I also send you."* The Father sent Jesus, and he received His apostolic commission from Him. Modern-day apostles receive their apostolic commission from Jesus.

In the New Testament there are other apostles apart from Paul: Barnabas, James the brother of Jesus, and many others – over twenty of them.

Next are prophets. These have already been defined at the beginning of this book.

Then come evangelists. The word "evangelist" means, "the one who preaches the good news". Evangelists preach Christ, salvation, and they manifest healings and miracles as an attestation. The primary call of an evangelist is to the lost. He has an external ministry in that he reaches out to the world to bring in a harvest of souls. Since evangelists preach the good news, most of their messages are christocentric and "soteriological", which means that they pertain to salvation.
An example in the New Testament is that of Philip, in Acts 8. We are told in verses 1 to 5 that Philip went to Samaria, and the Bible says he preached Christ and did miracles and healings. Evangelists have the anointing to heal the sick and do a lot of signs and wonders. Apostles and prophets also perform miracles in their ministries.

The word "pastor" (*poimen* in the Greek) or shepherd is used only once in the New Testament, but it can be seen in various synonyms, like the word "elder". The word *episkopos* or "bishop", can also be translated as a "pastor", "shepherd" or "overseer". A pastor primarily is a stationary minister. The pastor stays in the church and nurtures his flock. He teaches them (the "feeding") and tends them (cares for them and looks into their problems).

In Jeremiah 3:15, God said:

> *"And I will give you shepherds according to My heart, who will feed you with knowledge and understanding".*

A pastor who does not know how to teach the Bible is not qualified to be a pastor. Pastors must be able to teach and feed, otherwise all their flock will become skinny and will die spiritually. Pastors also attend to the hurting members of their flock with their counselling ministry, which is part of the pastoral ministry. Visiting his members, caring for them and being concerned for their problems, are all part of the work of a pastor. If anyone says he is a pastor, and he doesn't do these things, then he might not be called to be a pastor.

For teachers, the Greek word is *didaskalos*, from which we get the word "didactic", that is, to deduce. Teachers have the ability to make clear the Word of God, resulting in application in real life. They can take a difficult passage of scripture and break it down; they have the anointing to take mysteries and make them clear. Not everybody has that teaching anointing, not even other church leaders.

9b.   Qualifications of ministry gifts

The question here is, "What makes somebody qualified for ministry?" As I have said earlier, knowledge of God's word is primary for God's representatives. Let's look at Malachi 2:7:

> *"For the lips of a priest should keep knowledge, and people should seek the law from his mouth; for he is the messenger of the LORD of hosts."*

Those with the ministry gifts must know the Bible so well, that when

126

asked a question, they should not say, "Wait, tomorrow I will give you an answer", but there and then, they should be able to speak the Word of God. They must know God's Word in and out, so that they are ready to give an answer at any time (1 Peter 3:15).

If you are not well versed in the scriptures, you are not qualified to be a man of God. In Hosea 4:6, there is a warning for the priest: the Bible says:

> "... because you have rejected knowledge, I also will reject you from being priest for Me; because you have forgotten the law of your God, I also will forget your children."

The Bible also says in Hosea 4:6, *"My people are destroyed for lack of knowledge."* Paul also says in 1 Timothy 2:5-7:

> *"For there is one God and one Mediator between God and men, the Man Christ Jesus, who gave Himself a ransom for all, to be testified in due time, for which I was appointed a preacher and an apostle—I am speaking the truth in Christ and not lying—a teacher of the Gentiles in faith and truth."*

Paul said that he was first a preacher. All those with ministry gifts start in ministry as a preacher. You cannot start in ministry as a teacher if you are not well experienced, for teaching requires even more experience than preaching.

2 Timothy 1:11 says the same thing:

> "... to which I was appointed a preacher, an apostle, and a teacher of the Gentiles."

We are told by various scriptures in the book of Timothy how we must study the Word, and that the Word was inspired by God.

The ministry gifts also come with supernatural endowment. These are called Gifts of the Spirit, and they vary with the ministry gifts. For instance, in the prophetic office, the prophet has tools or equipment for his ministry.

A prophet normally has supernatural equipment called Revelation Gifts. These are the gifts that reveal something, because they know things supernaturally, before they are even told. These gifts are: the Gift of the Word of Wisdom, Word of Knowledge, Discerning of Spirits, and Prophecy. These are basic, though the mandatory gifts for the prophet are the Word of Knowledge and Gift of Prophecy.

Some prophets will have more of the Word of Wisdom than others. This is the ability to make very sharp predictions. Some will have the Gift of Discerning of Spirits, with which they will be able to see into the spirit world (for example, they may go to and fro to heaven through open visions). Other prophets will have the Gift of Miracles, Gift of Healings, Gift of Faith, and so on.

Some apostles also have Gifts of Healing. For instance, Elijah and Elisha healed people and saw miracles in their ministry. Apostles also have their anointings. We are told in 2 Corinthians 12:12 of the signs of an apostle, which are signs, wonders and mighty deeds. They can raise the dead, they can raise the crippled from the ground, and they can do so many other miraculous things.

Evangelists also have miracles and healings, and pastors and teachers may not particularly have any sensational gifts operating in their ministry, though some do.

The next thing we need to know about ministry gifts, is that they must have a proper order. Mark 3:13-15 says concerning Christ:

> *"And He went up on the mountain and called to Him those He Himself wanted. And they came to Him. Then He appointed twelve, that they might be with Him and that He might send them out to preach, and to have power to heal sicknesses and to cast out demons."*

The first reason why God calls men of God, whether they may be apostles, prophets, evangelists, pastors and teachers, is that, like other Christians, God wants to have fellowship with them. They must never sacrifice their quiet time, bible studies, devotion or prayer life. You cannot be a man of God and be so busy that you don't have time for God... very soon you will cease to be a man of God! When you have not seen God's face, you will have nothing to tell the people but your own message: you will end up leading the people astray.

One reason for which Jesus called the apostles, was that they might be with Him (Mark 3:14). And being with Him has to do with fellowship with Him. It has to do with studying the Bible to transform one's own character, and to be able to teach and divide the scriptures well for one's flock. Men of God must also pray to hear from God, through what we call "prophetic listening", that is, receiving direction from God on a daily basis concerning where one must and must not go; and concerning what must be preached and what must not be preached.

Apart from calling the apostles to be with Him, Jesus called them so that He might send them out to preach (Mark 3:14). We see that our first priority should be to have fellowship with Jesus. After that, we can go out to preach. Thirdly and lastly, as Mark 3:15 says, Jesus sends us out to have power to heal sicknesses and to cast out demons. This means that signs and wonders, what many people are focusing their attention on, is the last on the list.

In short, the man of God must first have fellowship with God. Secondly, God dispatches him with a message to give to the people. Thirdly, the word that is preached has to be confirmed with signs and wonders.

I have seen many countries where the highest value is placed on signs and wonders, and sometimes there is no preaching at all. That is not the plan of God.

Jesus gave us an example to follow, in Matthew 4:23:

"And Jesus went about all Galilee, teaching in their synagogues,

129

preaching the gospel of the kingdom, and healing all kinds of sickness and all kinds of disease among the people."

Here, the healing did not come first: the preaching did.

Let's look at Luke 5:16:

"So He Himself often withdrew into the wilderness and prayed."

Jesus had a strong prayer life: he always communed with the Father, often praying all night long, as we see in Luke 6:12, for instance:

"Now it came to pass in those days that He went out to the mountain to pray, and continued all night in prayer to God."

Likewise, a man of God must be very prayerful. He must spend time in the night to pray, to seek the face of God for his people. Though Jesus was a prophet (in Deuteronomy 18:18, Moses prophesied that a prophet will arise from the midst of the Jews), He gave place to preaching and teaching.

Some people say that prophets do not need to preach and teach; they only need to prophesy. That is false. We are told in Matthew 4:23:

"And Jesus went about all Galilee, teaching in their synagogues, preaching the gospel of the kingdom, and healing all kinds of sickness and all kinds of disease among the people."

9c.   *Three phases of a ministry gift*

There are three phases of a ministry gift. Whether a person is going to be an apostle, prophet, evangelist, pastor or teacher, his life will develop in three phases: the Call, the Preparation, and the Commission.

As I have already stated, many young men and women around the world receive their call from God, but they don't prepare themselves. They just step out and begin to function. They make a lot of mistakes because they are not educated in the things of God, and they end up leading a lot of people astray.

After the Call and the Preparation, the Commissioning comes when the individual is ready to go out and function. This is similar to the case of would-be medical doctors who have just finished medical school. Even after having studied medicine for seven years, they cannot start treating patients until they have been certified and licensed. They may hold the surgical instruments, but they are not allowed to use them to cut patients. So if this is what pertains in the natural, how much more with prophets who function like spiritual doctors? When spiritual doctors practise without finishing school, or worse – without ever having been to school - they will kill people spiritually.

Let us look at the commissioning of Jeremiah, in Jeremiah 1:1-10:

> "The words of Jeremiah the son of Hilkiah, of the priests who were in Anathoth in the land of Benjamin, to whom the word of the LORD came in the days of Josiah the son of Amon, king of Judah, in the thirteenth year of his reign. It came also in the days of Jehoiakim the son of Josiah, king of Judah, until the end of the eleventh year of Zedekiah the son of Josiah, king of Judah, until the carrying away of Jerusalem captive in the fifth month. Then the word of the LORD came to me, saying:
> "Before I formed you in the womb I knew you; Before you were born I sanctified you; I ordained you a prophet to the nations." Then said I: "Ah, Lord GOD! Behold, I cannot speak, for I am a youth." But the LORD said to me: "Do not say, 'I am a youth,' For you shall go to all to whom I send you, And whatever I command you, you shall speak.
>
> Do not be afraid of their faces, For I am with you to deliver you," says the LORD. Then the LORD put forth His hand and touched my mouth, and the LORD said to me: "Behold, I have put My words in

your mouth. See, I have this day set you over the nations and over the kingdoms, To root out and to pull down, To destroy and to throw down, To build and to plant."

The words *"... I have this day set you over..."* indicate that this is the day of Jeremiah's commission. Jeremiah's father was a priest; the family lived in a place called Anathoth. As a boy, Jeremiah must have been serving in the priesthood: he must have served his father for many years.

God told Jeremiah that he had already called him before he was born. So, the call may come very early in life; even before we are born. But that does not mean that we are ready for ministry. Jeremiah prepared: he was first a priest, before becoming a prophet. He studied and sought the face of the Lord, and God set him in the prophetic office at the appropriate time.

9d. The role of the New Testament Prophets

In this section, I want us to look at the supernatural equipment of the prophets. This involves the powers used by the prophets, and the anointing upon them.

There are nine Gifts of the Spirit in the New Testament, listed in 1 Corinthians 12. These gifts are split into three categories: the revelation gifts, power gifts, and the vocal or utterance gifts. The revelation gifts are gifts that reveal things; the power gifts are gifts that do things; vocal or utterance gifts are gifts that say things.

As stated earlier, prophets have revelations. They can see things supernaturally. Once I was preaching in a certain place with a large wall: I could not see outside. I said to a lady in the meeting, "You have a white car and you are 47 years". She said, "Yes, how did you know?" I told her that I could see her car parked in the car park, behind the wall. This is something I saw in the Spirit. We call it spiritual vision.

How do the gifts operate? Let's look at them one-by-one, starting with the Gift of the Word of Wisdom.

i.   The Gift of the Word of Wisdom

This is the supernatural ability to know by revelation, the plans and purposes of God for the future, for people, places and nations. Sometimes this gift also reveals the plans of the devil, so that we can avert them. This is the gift that brings prediction – the foretelling of events.

This wisdom is not ordinary wisdom for life. There are different kinds of wisdom. For instance, there is human wisdom: this is the kind of wisdom people have to design cars and aeroplanes. That is not the Gift of the Word of Wisdom, which is a spiritual gift only available to born-again people filled with the Holy Ghost.

Through the Word of Wisdom, God gives "a word", a little fraction or fragment of the things that God is doing in the universe. This wisdom is different from the kind of wisdom that God gave to Solomon, for instance. Solomon's wisdom was the wisdom to make right decisions in life. In James 1:5, we are told, *"If anyone lacks wisdom, let him ask God…"*.

We are told in 1 Corinthians 12:11 that the spiritual gifts are distributed by the Holy Spirit, as the Holy Spirit wills. So, for instance, if you are not a prophet, you may not have the Gift of the Word of Wisdom. God may not anoint you to see into the future, since that is not your calling.

If scripture says in 1 Corinthians 12:11, that the Holy Spirit distributes the gifts according to His will, then this would contradict James 1:5 that says anybody can ask for wisdom. The two types of wisdom are therefore clearly different. In Matthew 10:16 for instance, Jesus says:

> *"Behold, I send you out as sheep in the midst of wolves. Therefore be wise as serpents and harmless as doves."*

An example of the Word of Wisdom can be seen in Acts 11:27-30:

"During this time some prophets came down from Jerusalem to Antioch. One of them, named Agabus, stood up and through the Spirit predicted that a severe famine would spread over the entire Roman world. (This happened during the reign of Claudius.) The disciples, each according to his ability, decided to provide help for the brothers living in Judea. This they did, sending their gift to the elders by Barnabas and Saul."

The prophet Agabus prophesied that there was going to be a famine. At the time he spoke, there might have even been a bounteous harvest. In response, the people decided to gather some food and prepare.

ii.   *The Gift of the Word of Knowledge*

The word of knowledge implies two basic things. Firstly, a word is a fragment or a piece of information. Secondly there are different kinds of knowledge. There is the knowledge of the bible, but this is not the gift of the word of knowledge. Again we have natural knowledge of 'a priori' events. This indicates events known to us in advance. We can acquire knowledge by studying various subjects but all this will not constitute the gift of the word of knowledge. The gift of the word of knowledge is essentially supernatural. It is a revelation of certain facts in the mind of God, which will lie in the domain of the past and the present. God is omniscient, that is to say that He is all knowing, but He will on certain occasions reveal some facts about people, places, nations etc. The prophets have this ability on a continuous basis. Now there is the need to for us to understand the meaning of the word revelation for emphases. The Word revelation is derived from the Greek verb *apokalupto*. It means to unveil a mystery .A mystery is a hidden truth. Imagine one enters a room with a transparent box covered with a thick cloth. Suppose there is a stone in the box before the person arrived in the room. The fact is that the stone may have been in the box many days, but the moment the cloth is taken away the observer sees it for the first time, this is the concept of revelation. We will now look at certain passages in both the old and new testaments to explain the concept in a more concrete way.

134

In Samuel chapter 9,we have an account of the missing donkeys of Kish, the father of Saul. Saul was sent by his father to go and look for his lost asses. He set out on his journey with his servant. after a fruitless search they were told they could go and enquire from the famous prophet Samuel. The Hebrews were very familiar with the ministry of the prophet. They will not do anything without consulting the prophet. Even Kings went to enquire of prophets, before they went to war. The people generally did not have the Holy Spirit unlike us in the New Testament. We do not need to seek out prophets now for guidance. In any case Samuel told Saul when they met that the donkeys had already been found three days before. The fact is that there may have been many donkeys that must have been lost in Israel on this occasion, but God revealed that of Saul because; He had a plan to reveal His greater plan of enstooling him as the first king in Israel. This means the prophet did not have knowledge of all lost donkeys at the time except that which was unveiled to him. He later told him about God's plan. We have another example in the New Testament in John chapter 4.

This is the encounter of Jesus and the Samaritan woman at Jacob's well. The Lord asked the woman to go and bring her husband. She replied that she does not have a husband. Jesus said, she had had five husbands and the one she was living with at the time was not her husband. The woman exclaimed that Jesus must be a prophet. This is because Jesus had no access to this knowledge except by supernatural means.

The Old Testament writing prophets usually started writing their books by saying the word of the Lord came to them. A Prophet will suddenly become aware instantaneously, that certain information had been inserted into his mind. The revelation is actually passed to his spirit by the Holy Spirit who indwells the Prophet. The message is instantaneously transferred to his mind and he becomes aware. (See Nehemiah 9:30, 1 Peter 1:9-12, Job 32:8).

I have personally been used in the gift of word of knowledge for the past 26 years.

On many occasions when ministering I will suddenly know how old an individual was, his name, sometimes his profession, name of home town, and other factual knowledge. I will sometimes be able to tell by the Spirit what is going on in peoples lives, I will sometimes know and repeat certain conversations a husband had had with his wife before coming to my meeting. Frequently I will suddenly know what their ministry calling is and their gifts what God has endowed them with and they will be accurate.

As discussed earlier, the gift of the Word of Knowledge is a supernatural revelation of facts in the mind of God, about people, places and nations, past and present. Some of the people who operate the Word of Knowledge, do so through familiar spirits: since these spirits are familiar with people, places and things, they can transfer information to people about what is currently happening, or what has already happened. But many times, these spirits cannot tell what will happen in the future, which is the mind of God.

That is why Ephesians 3:10 says:

"…to the intent that now the manifold wisdom of God might be made known by the church to the principalities and powers in the heavenly places."

This means that the Church knows some secrets that demonic powers do not know. One thing I have noticed is that people who cannot prophesy the mind of God concerning the future of people, places and nations, normally may not be operating in the Spirit of God. Those who are always speaking about the present and the past could be suspect. That does not mean that true prophets cannot speak of the present and the past, but this is one way by which one can differentiate between true and false prophets.

When false prophets prophesy about the future, they talk about negative things in the future – disasters, which the Devil himself has planned. God does not plan accidents, though He knows everything that is going to happen, and He permits certain things to happen.

An example of the Word of Knowledge can be seen in John 4:11-19, during the encounter between the Samaritan woman and Jesus.

> *"'Sir," the woman said, "you have nothing to draw with and the well is deep. Where can you get this living water? Are you greater than our father Jacob, who gave us the well and drank from it himself, as did also his sons and his flocks and herds?"*
>
> *Jesus answered, "Everyone who drinks this water will be thirsty again, but whoever drinks the water I give him will never thirst. Indeed, the water I give him will become in him a spring of water welling up to eternal life."*
>
> *The woman said to him, "Sir, give me this water so that I won't get thirsty and have to keep coming here to draw water."*
>
> *He told her, "Go, call your husband and come back."*
>
> *"I have no husband," she replied.*
>
> *Jesus said to her, "You are right when you say you have no husband. The fact is, you have had five husbands, and the man you now have is not your husband. What you have just said is quite true."*
>
> *"Sir," the woman said, "I can see that you are a prophet."*

The people of that time knew about the prophetic office. Jesus revealed to the Samaritan woman that in the past she had had five husbands. How did Jesus know this? This was the Word of Knowledge in operation, which operates today in the prophetic office.

I frequently operate the gift of the Word of Knowledge. For example, I might say to a lady I had never met or spoken with before, "You have three children, and the first is a boy". This is the supernatural gift of the World of Knowledge in operation.

iii.   *The Gift of Discerning of Spirits*

The Gift of Discerning of Spirits is the supernatural ability to see into the spiritual realm. To discern something is to know something either by seeing or hearing in the spirit world. There are three kinds of spirits: God the Spirit; spirit beings – good and evil angels (fallen angels, including Satan); and the human spirit. Any class of spirits can be discerned.

Jesus can be seen (He is the only member of the Godhead who can be seen in bodily form, according to Colossians 2:9. The Holy Spirit can be seen in similitudes as, for instance, the seven fires before the throne of God; or as a dove, as John the Baptist saw (John 1:32-34); but we cannot discern the Holy Spirit in bodily form, as with Jesus. The Father cannot be seen at all, according to 1 Timothy 6:16:

"...who alone is immortal and who lives in unapproachable light, whom no one has seen or can see. To him be honour and might forever. Amen."

We can also hear voices in the spirit world. I know people who have gone to the throne room of God, in heaven, and heard God's voice from a cloud, though they did not see him.

John, on the Isle of Patmos, had a lot of revelations in the form of visions. He was operating this prophetic Gift of Discerning of Spirits. I will say that John was an apostolic prophet. Daniel, on the other hand, was a visionary prophet. He also had in the operation of his ministry, this Gift of Discerning of Spirits. Sometimes people with the Gift of Discerning of Spirits can see the spirits that are causing disease in people's bodies.

There are three different kinds of visions. Spiritual vision is the lowest level. An example of spiritual vision is when, while preaching, I can see with the eyes of my spirit, a car parked behind the church building. The next kind of spiritual vision is a trance. This is when a person sees into the spirit world, and the entire physical environment is suspended. For instance, Peter had a trance before preaching to Cornelius' household (Acts 10:9-16).

In a trance, all the things around you will vanish. You may not see items around you, such as tables and chairs, but you will be more conscious of the spirit world. The highest form of vision is open vision, where your physical senses are not suspended, and your spiritual senses are brought into focus. In other words, you can be standing in a place, seeing the chairs around you, and yet you also see an angel appearing to you in bodily form, like a human being.

138

For an example of the Gift of Discerning of Spirits. let's look at Acts 23:11:

> *"The following night the Lord stood near Paul and said, "Take courage! As you have testified about me in Jerusalem, so you must also testify in Rome."*

Here, Paul actually saw Jesus, who gave him a message for the future, about the purpose and plan of God to be fulfilled in Rome.

iv. *The Gift of Prophecy*

Every prophet has the Gift of Prophecy. This is a supernatural utterance in a known language, where the speaker speaks the mind of God at the impulse of the moment. In 1 Corinthians 14:3,the Bible declares, that he who prophesies speaks to men for edification, exhortation and comfort.

v. *The Gifts of Tongues and Interpretation of Tongues*

Some prophets also have the Gift of Tongues and the Gift of Interpretation of Tongues. I have those gifts, which are equivalent to prophecy, as they entail speaking in tongues and interpreting what is being spoken. Prophecy comes out of the interpretation, and something might be revealed.

Chapter 10:

What the Bible Says about False Prophets

The beginning of the prophetic movement dates back to the very beginning of creation. We are told in Jude 14, that Enoch the seventh from Adam prophesied about apostates in the last days. As early as Genesis 20:7, we learn, that the patriarch Abraham was a prophet. In Luke 1:70,we are told, that God spoke by the mouth of His holy prophets who have been, since the world began. In the book of Deuteronomy chapter 18: 9-22, Moses admonishes the Israelites not to inherit the wicked customs of the Canaanites whose land they were to inherit. He particularly warned them against any involvement with the occult. There was a kind of 'pseudo' prophetic ministry in the surrounding heathen nations as well as in the land of Canaan. They were involved in demon trafficking, spiritism, necromancy, witchcraft, divination and the like. They prophesied by demonic deities and of course they did not know the God of heaven. Inasmuch as God had His true spokesmen or prophets, there have always been false prophets in manifestation through out the Old Testament era and the New Testament period to this day. The very fact that the bible frequently uses the adjective holy when describing His true prophets, is an indication that there are also unholy prophets. The determination of a false prophetic status has largely been misconstrued in the church today. A lot of well meaning Christians can seldom make that determination. In the light of several divine warnings in the bible, one cannot take this subject lightly. For instance, in Deuteronomy 13:1-5,the bible declares that if a prophet arose or a dreamer of dreams and gave a sign, and the sign did come to pass, and afterward he attempted to lead the people away from the true worship of Yahweh that prophet was to be put to death. One can see immediately from this text that a false prophet is not determined by his prophetic accuracy or by the spectacular signs he may perform. Indeed we are warned in 2 Thessalonians 2:9, that the coming of the lawless one will be according to the working of Satan, and will be attended by remarkable signs and lying wonders. The lesson is that we do not determine the status of a prophet merely by the spiritual gifts they may manifest. There are more important issues to consider before that. In Matthew 7:15, Jesus made a profound statement with regard to this. He told His disciples to beware of false prophets, and that they will know them by their fruits. This intimates that a person may be a true prophesier but a false prophet. Thus a false prophet is determined by his state of being. The bottom line is his conformation to the image of Christ. We will take up this matter in detail as we progress. In the Olivet discourse of our Lord He issued a warning, that getting to the end of time many false prophets will arise and deceive many. In 2 Peter 2:1-3, we find the apostle making reference to the fact that there were false prophets in the Old Testament period. False prophets can bring destruction to the people of God; it is no wonder that the scriptures are full of divine warnings concerning their presence in the assembly of God. This makes it a very cogent reason to undertake a study to discover, who a false prophet is, what they do, how to identify them, how the church can be shielded from them, and also how they came about that status and more importantly, if there is hope, how they can be redeemed to become true. These will be the preoccupation of this section, and to these answers we now turn.

Going back to Matthew 7:15-23, Jesus warned that the church should beware of false prophets who come as wolves in sheep's clothing. It is clear that the statement is metaphorical. Looking at the symbolism, one can see that a wolf is a ferocious animal that will easily tear the pray apart. Secondly, for a wolf to disguise as a sheep, it means it wants to creep in among sheep unnoticed and in the process do as much damage as possible. Again the fruits of the false prophet will determine his status.

There are two kinds of fruits to observe. The fruit of their ministries and their lives. We have to check if their doctrine is sound, whether they are able to teach and preach nothing but the truth. We need to know whether they qualify for the high office of Christian leadership.(

see 1 Timothy 3:1-7, Titus 1:5-9).We need to look at their ministerial ethics, their depth of understanding with respect to the things of God. After checking these things we will now look at their gifting, whether they are valid. We have to test for maturity, prophetic accuracy, prophetic etiquette, and many more.

We need to understand here that an individual will be false if heaven does not recognize him as true. In other words, we need the divine perspective on any one who claims to be a prophet. Thankfully in many cases the matter can be decided without making a divine enquiry but by consulting the logos or the written word, since therein lies the mind of Christ. In Matthew 21:25, Jesus posed a question. He asked the Pharisees whether John's baptism or essentially John's prophetic office was from heaven or from men. This means there are people holding titles which heaven does not recognize. For example in Revelation 2:18, Jesus rebukes the church of Thyatira for entertaining a woman by the name Jezebel who called herself a prophetess but was not. Two things Jesus pointed out with regards to her false status were her false teaching and her false lifestyle.

This book does not seek to be judgmental, but to enlighten the church in the light of divine warnings. Indeed the church should seek to redeem her own who may have degenerated to false prophetic status, and confront the agents of Satan, peradventure they themselves might be saved. We should all be aware of our fallibility so long as we remain in our mortal bodies and so help our brethren who may have missed it in this area and not condemn them. We are all to work out our salvation with fear and trembling. The bible says in Galatians 6:1,2 that if any one is overtaken in a trespass, we who are spiritual should restore such a one in the spirit of gentleness, considering that we can also be tempted. We are to bear one another's burden.

Due to divine warnings given to the Old Testament assembly and the New Testament Church, the Church must know thoroughly who a false prophet is, in order to avoid deception.

As said earlier, false prophets may use counterfeit gifts, which are not from God. If a prophet who is true, gives a word, which is not accurate or true, and it does not come to pass, that does not mean that he is a false prophet. A false prophet is not necessarily one who gives false prophecy. Of course, false prophets often give false prophecies, but that is not what makes them false per se. A false prophet is known by his status, by what he is. That is what makes him false.

True prophets sometimes give false prophecies. For instance, we know in the Old Testament that Samuel, a true prophet, once gave a false prophecy when he went to anoint one of the sons of Jesse to be king. He first went to anoint the firstborn, Eliab, and he got it wrong. It was rather the lastborn, David, whom God had anointed. Samuel missed it, because he looked at the outside. That is why God said in 1 Samuel 16:7 that He does not look at the outside, but He looks at the heart.

There are many references to false prophets in the Bible, because as said earlier, false prophets deceive God's people – they bring about deception in general. So there are many warnings in both the Old the New Testaments: let's look at some of them.

10a.   Divine warnings in the Scriptures

Deuteronomy 13:1-5 states:

> "If a prophet, or one who foretells by dreams, appears among you and announces to you a miraculous sign or wonder, and if the sign or wonder of which he has spoken takes place, and he says, "Let us follow other gods" (gods you have not known) "and let us worship them," you must not listen to the words of that prophet or dreamer. The LORD your God is testing you to find out whether you love him with all your heart and with all your soul. It is the LORD your God you must follow, and him you must revere. Keep his commands and obey him; serve him and hold fast to him. That prophet or dreamer must be put to death, because he preached rebellion against the LORD your God, who brought you out of Egypt and redeemed you from the land of slavery; he has tried to turn

you from the way the LORD your God commanded you to follow. You must purge the evil from among you."

Here, we see a false prophet giving a true prophecy. We know he is false because he leads the people of God away from God, either through his teaching or by his way of life. He makes them go astray.

Let's go to 1 John 4:1-3. Here, the Bible says:

"Dear friends, do not believe every spirit, but test the spirits to see whether they are from God, because many false prophets have gone out into the world. This is how you can recognize the Spirit of God: Every spirit that acknowledges that Jesus Christ has come in the flesh is from God, but every spirit that does not acknowledge Jesus is not from God. This is the spirit of the antichrist, which you have heard is coming and even now is already in the world."

2 Peter 2:1-3 states:

"But there were also false prophets among the people, just as there will be false teachers among you. They will secretly introduce destructive heresies, even denying the sovereign Lord who bought them—bringing swift destruction on themselves. Many will follow their shameful ways and will bring the way of truth into disrepute. In their greed these teachers will exploit you with stories they have made up. Their condemnation has long been hanging over them, and their destruction has not been sleeping."

False prophets will bring heresies, which are wrong teachings. One mark of false prophets is that they are covetous, and as such, they are greedy for money. They therefore do many things because of money. They say nice things so that people give them money. They never bring the counsel of God; they never show you the right way, truth and life. God is going to judge them eventually.

In Matthew 7:15-20, we read:

"Watch out for false prophets. They come to you in sheep's clothing, but inwardly they are ferocious wolves. By their fruit you will recognize them.

Do people pick grapes from thorn bushes, or figs from thistles? Likewise every good tree bears good fruit, but a bad tree bears bad fruit. A good tree cannot bear bad fruit, and a bad tree cannot bear good fruit. Every tree that does not bear good fruit is cut down and thrown into the fire. Thus, by their fruit you will recognize them."

Jesus says we will not recognise false prophets by how good or bad their prophecies are, but by their lifestyle. He went on to say in Matthew 7:21-23:

"Not everyone who says to me, 'Lord, Lord,' will enter the kingdom of heaven, but only he who does the will of my Father who is in heaven. Many will say to me on that day, 'Lord, Lord, did we not prophesy in your name, and in your name drive out demons and perform many miracles?' Then I will tell them plainly, 'I never knew you. Away from me, you evildoers!"

Let's look at 2 Timothy 3:13:

"…evil men and impostors will go from bad to worse, deceiving and being deceived."

People who are false are actually impostors: they present themselves as sound people, but they are not. The Bible says that the evil men and impostors will grow worse and worse in the last days. They will be deceiving people while they themselves are being deceived by Satan. This means that some of them do not even know that what they are doing is wrong.

Jesus gives a warning in Matthew 24:11:

"…many false prophets will appear and deceive many people."

The issue of deception keeps coming up. The word deceive means "believing a lie" - people are told something which is not true. From my own research, I found that there are three different kinds of false prophets:

i.   *Non-Christian sorcerers or mediums.*

These people are not Christians at all; they are not born-again. They are servants of Satan. Look at Acts 13:4-12:

> *"The two of them, sent on their way by the Holy Spirit, went down to Seleucia and sailed from there to Cyprus. When they arrived at Salamis, they proclaimed the word of God in the Jewish synagogues. John was with them as their helper.*
> *They traveled through the whole island until they came to Paphos. There they met a Jewish sorcerer and false prophet named Bar-Jesus, who was an attendant of the proconsul, Sergius Paulus. The proconsul, an intelligent man, sent for Barnabas and Saul because he wanted to hear the word of God. But Elymas the sorcerer (for that is what his name means) opposed them and tried to turn the proconsul from the faith. Then Saul, who was also called Paul, filled with the Holy Spirit, looked straight at Elymas and said, "You are a child of the devil and an enemy of everything that is right! You are full of all kinds of deceit and trickery. Will you never stop perverting the right ways of the Lord? Now the hand of the Lord is against you. You are going to be blind, and for a time you will be unable to see the light of the sun."*
> *Immediately mist and darkness came over him, and he groped about, seeking someone to lead him by the hand. When the proconsul saw what had happened, he believed, for he was amazed at the teaching about the Lord."*

Paul encountered a false prophet. This man was not only a non-Christian, but he was also a sorcerer. The Bible says that this false prophet sought to turn the proconsul away from the faith.

ii. Christians with the prophetic gift who are not trained or prepared for the prophetic office.

They are not set in the office by God, so they are false. 1 Corinthians 12:28 says:

"And in the church God has appointed first of all apostles, second prophets, third teachers, then workers of miracles, also those having gifts of healing, those able to help others, those with gifts of administration, and those speaking in different kinds of tongues."

If God has not set anyone as a prophet, than that person is a false prophet.

iii. Christian leaders usurping the prophetic office.

It is dangerous to stand in an office to which one has not been called. A genuine man of God might try to be a prophet by all means, even though God has not called him to be a prophet. If he moves out of his office and strives to be a prophet, he will become a false prophet, because he has not got the status of a true prophet by God.

Therefore, it is dangerous to stand in an office to which one has not been called. The grace of God may eventually depart, and one can lose God's covering, possibly resulting in degeneration of character, financial hardship, and manipulation by occult powers.

10b.   Characteristics of false prophets

Most of the characteristics of false prophets can also be found in Christians; some of these traits can be found in young Christians who have the prophetic gift, but are not yet prophets – they move out of the will of God. They eventually begin to manifest very dangerous and bad character.

i.   They *deceive God's people* (see 2 Timothy 3:13).

ii.   They themselves are deceived for *lack of knowledge* (see Matthew 22:29 and Isaiah 8:20).

iii. The *fruits and life of ministry of a false prophet are questionable.*

This refers to what we see of a false prophet's lifestyle. Some of them are into money laundering; some are cocaine dealers, or are found praying for cocaine dealers to carry cocaine: these are all shady – they are false (see Matthew 7:15).

Many times also, false prophets love money. 1 Timothy 6:6-16 warns against the love of money:

> *"But godliness with contentment is great gain. For we brought nothing into the world, and we can take nothing out of it. But if we have food and clothing, we will be content with that. People who want to get rich fall into temptation and a trap and into many foolish and harmful desires that plunge men into ruin and destruction. For the love of money is a root of all kinds of evil. Some people, eager for money, have wandered from the faith and pierced themselves with many griefs. But you, man of God, flee from all this, and pursue righteousness, godliness, faith, love, endurance and gentleness. Fight the good fight of the faith. Take hold of the eternal life to which you were called when you made your good confession in the presence of many witnesses. In the sight of God, who gives life to everything, and of Christ Jesus, who while testifying before Pontius Pilate made the good confession, I charge you to keep this command without spot or blame until the appearing of our Lord Jesus Christ, which God will bring about in his own time—God, the blessed and only Ruler, the King of kings and Lord of lords, who alone is immortal and who lives in unapproachable light, whom no one has seen or can see. To him be honour and might forever. Amen."*

Micah 2:6-11 also tells us about false prophetic ministry. In this passage, God was speaking about the Israelites: they preferred going to false prophets than true prophets (even to the extent of telling true prophets not to prattle, that is, not to preach!), so they themselves were living in sin:

> *"Do not prophesy," their prophets say. "Do not prophesy about these things; disgrace will not overtake us." Should it be said, O house of Jacob: "Is the Spirit of the LORD angry? Does he do such things?"*

149

"Do not my words do good to him whose ways are upright?
Lately my people have risen up like an enemy. You strip off the rich
robe from those who pass by without a care, like men returning from
battle. You drive the women of my people from their pleasant homes.
You take away my blessing from their children forever.
Get up, go away! For this is not your resting place, because it is defiled,
it is ruined, beyond all remedy. If a liar and deceiver comes and says, 'I
will prophesy for you plenty of wine and beer,' He would be just the
prophet for this people!"

False prophets talk about nice things; in other words, they do not talk
about sin or God's judgement. They encourage people to do what they
want, as if that is all right. For this reason, many people do not like
true prophets, because they tell the truth. But I want to be true to God
– a genuine, right and good man of God all my life, so that I can be a
true model. That is my prayer.

Micah 3:5-11 states:

"This is what the LORD says: "As for the prophets who lead my
people astray, if one feeds them, they proclaim 'peace'; if he does not,
they prepare to wage war against him.
Therefore night will come over you, without visions, and darkness,
without divination. The sun will set for the prophets, and the day will
go dark for them.
The seers will be ashamed and the diviners disgraced. They will all cover
their faces because there is no answer from God." But as for me, I am
filled with power, with the Spirit of the LORD, and with justice and
might, to declare to Jacob his transgression, to Israel his sin.
Hear this, you leaders of the house of Jacob, you rulers of the house of
Israel, who despise justice and distort all that is right; Who build Zion
with bloodshed, and Jerusalem with wickedness.
Her leaders judge for a bribe, her priests teach for a price, and her
prophets tell fortunes for money. Yet they lean upon the LORD and
say, "Is not the LORD among us? No disaster will come upon us."

Micah says that these prophets prophesied good things to those who give them money, and bad things to those who did not give them money. Those kinds of prophecies are not from God. There shall be judgement for those prophets.

Micah, on the other hand, was a true prophet who told the people what God was saying, which was that they should repent of their sins. It meant that Micah was not popular, but God stood with him wherever he went.

Jesus was also a true prophet. He spent time with the rich and the poor alike – he met the needs of all. True prophets go to whomever they are sent. Elijah was sent to a poor widow in Zarephath, and he went. He too was a true prophet.

Jude 10-11 gives us more characteristics of false prophetic ministry:

> *"Yet these men speak abusively against whatever they do not understand; and what things they do understand by instinct, like unreasoning animals—these are the very things that destroy them.*
> *Woe to them! They have taken the way of Cain; they have rushed for profit into Balaam's error; they have been destroyed in Korah's rebellion."*

Balaam is used as an example here. He was a false prophet and he died because of his love for money. A prophet <u>must</u> stay away from the love of money. I, for instance, left a well-paying job in the US because of my prophetic ministry. I waited for God, and I know that God is going to bless me. I will never charge anything for prophesying. God freely gives the gifts to us.
If somebody chooses to bless a prophet out of their own free will, that is acceptable, but a prophet cannot say, "Give me this money before I give you a prophecy". We can teach about giving, and we can even raise funds for God's work, but we cannot force anyone to give us money.

Numbers 31 shows us the end of Balaam, and serves as an example to all of us in the prophetic ministry, so that we do not go astray.

Balaam was going to curse God's people, and he was warned by God not to go, but he still went. Eventually, he became apostate. Let's look at Numbers 31:1-8:

> *"The LORD said to Moses, "Take vengeance on the Midianites for the Israelites. After that, you will be gathered to your people."*
>
> *So Moses said to the people, "Arm some of your men to go to war against the Midianites and to carry out the LORD's vengeance on them. Send into battle a thousand men from each of the tribes of Israel." So twelve thousand men armed for battle, a thousand from each tribe, were supplied from the clans of Israel. Moses sent them into battle, a thousand from each tribe, along with Phinehas son of Eleazar, the priest, who took with him articles from the sanctuary and the trumpets for signaling.*
>
> *They fought against Midian, as the LORD commanded Moses, and killed every man. Among their victims were Evi, Rekem, Zur, Hur and Reba—the five kings of Midian. They also killed Balaam son of Beor with the sword."*

Consider Gehazi (2 Kings 5:1-27). He was a servant of Elisha, and because of the love of money, he became leprous – he and his descendants. A man called Naaman offered Elisha gifts after receiving healing through Elisha, but Elisha refused to take the gifts. Gehazi ran after Naaman, claiming that he had been sent to collect the gifts from Naaman. From that time on, Gehazi lost his calling.

iv. False prophets are manipulated by occult powers

False prophets are manipulated by demons. We see an example of this in 1 Kings 22:1-28. Micaiah the prophet stood before King Ahab, when Ahab wanted to go to war against Ramoth Gilead. Ahab, an occultist king whose wife was the evil queen Jezebel, called King Jehoshaphat, a good king, to go to war with him. Jehoshaphat asked for a prophet, so that they may enquire of the Lord.

400 false prophets were brought in and they began prophesying for Ahab. They only spoke the things Ahab wanted to hear. They

therefore prophesied that Ahab would win the war. Jehoshaphat, suspicious, still requested for a good prophet. Ahab told him that there was one prophet left, called Micaiah, but he complained that Micaiah never gave him good prophecies.

Micaiah was brought in, and he saw all Israel scattered and leader-less (meaning that Ahab would die in the battle). Micaiah was imprisoned for prophesying such a "bad" prophecy. But then the prophet had a vision where he saw the throne of God; God was seated with the angels in heaven, and evil spirits were also present in the heavenly meeting. God said, *"Who will entice Ahab into attacking Ramoth Gilead and go to his death there?"* Micaiah saw an evil spirit go before the throne of God, volunteering to become a lying spirit in the mouths of all Ahab's prophets.

Today, if a prophet is false, lying spirits may be using him, and he himself may not even know.

In all Christendom, talking about the history of the Church and the Old Testament, up until now, prophets who are true have been persecuted. One mark of a true prophet is his lack of popularity, because he brings messages that people do not want to hear. The Word of God says that true prophets confront our lifestyles and challenge us to live right for God. On the other hand, false prophets are very much liked, because they meet the desires of the people.

Luke 6:20-26 has blessings for true prophets and warnings for false prophets:

> *"Looking at his disciples, he said: "Blessed are you who are poor, for yours is the kingdom of God. Blessed are you who hunger now, for you will be satisfied. Blessed are you who weep now, for you will laugh. Blessed are you when men hate you, when they exclude you and insult you and reject your name as evil, because of the Son of Man.*
> *"Rejoice in that day and leap for joy, because great is your reward in heaven. For that is how their fathers treated the prophets. "But woe to you who are rich, for you have already received your comfort.*

Woe to you who are well fed now, for you will go hungry. Woe to you who laugh now, for you will mourn and weep. Woe to you when all men speak well of you, for that is how their fathers treated the false prophets"

ABOUT THE BOOK

It is true that the *logos* or written word of God is sufficient for living a successful Christian life. As such, the biblical revelation to mankind is the foundation of a solid walk with God.

God however endows some people with the gift of prophecy, the ability to reveal His mind. This gift is very powerful and precious, and the *rhema*, which is the prophetic word spoken at the impulse of the moment, could be as powerful and revealing as it is frightening, especially given occasional abuses.

"Prophecy and Prophets" is written largely as a response to the errors and misinterpretations, which has been besetting the prophetic movement since the early 1980s. It gives guidelines for verifying the truth or otherwise of prophetic utterances and for discerning the true prophetic vessels from the false ones.

ABOUT THE AUTHOR

Richard Oswald Commey holds a Bachelor's degree in Electrical Engineering, and has attained membership of the Institution of Electrical Engineers in the United Kingdom, through postgraduate examinations. He also holds a PhD in Biblical studies, specializing in prophecy. He has been working and researching in this field for the past 26 years.

Dr. Commey is the General Overseer of Ramah Chapel International, with branches in London, Ohio, and New Jersey. He is the president and founder of Ramah Prophetic ministries, an international prophetic outreach ministry. He is also a senior lecturer at South London Christian College, one of the premier theological colleges in the United Kingdom.

Dr. Commey is a seasoned prophet and teacher who has been called by the Lord to teach on the subject of prophecy and prophets, as well as demonstrating the prophetic gifts and activating ministries. He also mentors and builds up aspiring prophets, prophetesses, prophetic intercessors and prophetic believers in general. He has travelled extensively to many nations of the world, holding prophetic conferences in various churches. His prophecies concerning individuals, churches and even nations have a track record of dramatic fulfilment.

Dr. Commey is married to Babsi, who has been a great support to him in the ministry, and is herself a gifted minstrel in the vineyard. They have three children.

ABOUT CONTACT INFORMATION

ADDRESS:

Rev. Dr. Richard Oswald Commey
Ramah Prophetic Ministries
P.O.Box 2280
Ilford IG1 1EJ
UNITED KINGDOM

TEL: +447946707715 , +447983332175

E-MAIL: richcommey@yahoo.com

WEBSITE: www.lifestream.tv/ramah

Lightning Source UK Ltd.
Milton Keynes UK
UKOW02f1019191116

287991UK00001B/31/P